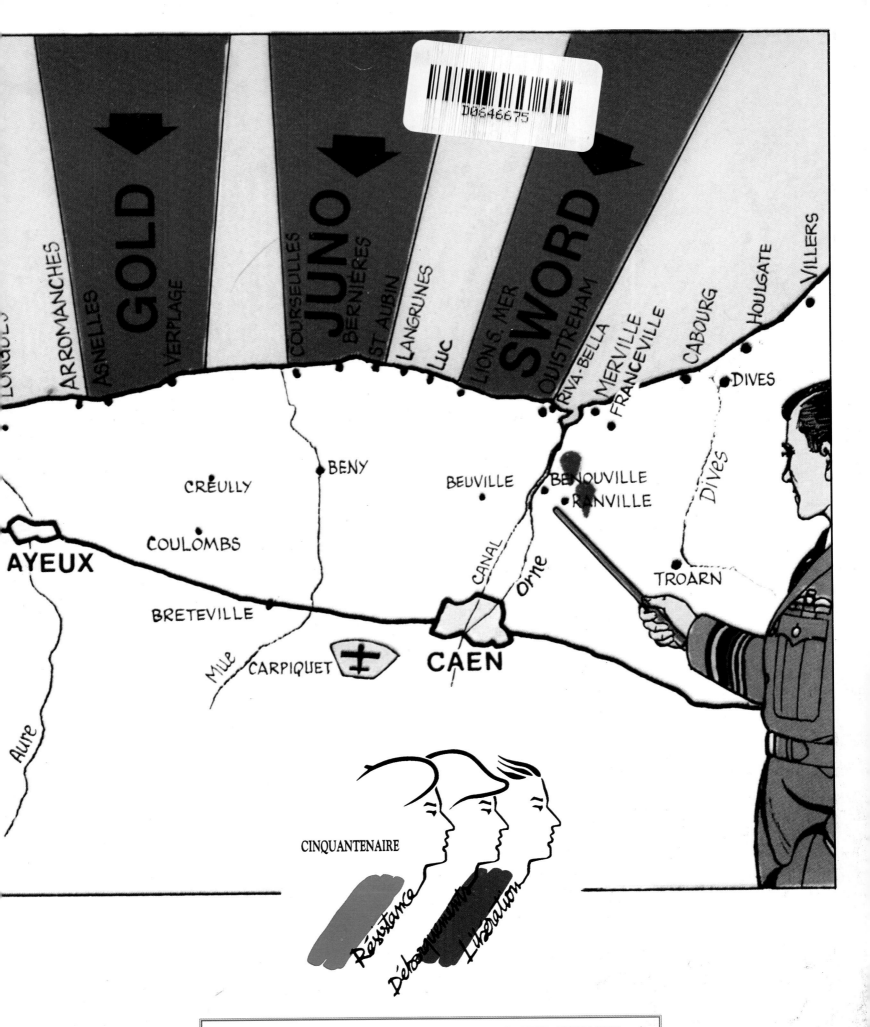

CINQUANTENAIRE

Résistance Débarquements Libération

THIS ALBUM HAS BEEN PUBLISHED UNDER
THE HIGH PATRONAGE OF THE FRENCH MISSION
FOR THE FIFTIETH ANNIVERSARY OF THE
LANDINGS AND THE LIBERATION OF FRANCE

D-DAY
OPERATION OVERLORD
JUNE 6TH, 1944

Script
Serge SAINT-MICHEL

Drawings
MISTER KIT

Colours
Martine BOUTIN

Historical counsellors
Isabelle BOURNIER and Rémy DESQUESNES

Publishers
Antoine CHAMPAIN, Richard GRUMBERG and Patrice le HODEY

MÉMOIRE D'EUROPE

P A R I S

> *In homage
> to the women and men,
> uniformed and civil,
> who gave so much
> for freedom.*
>
> **The Publisher**

This album has been printed specially in commemoration of the 50th anniversary of the June 6, 1944 D-DAY landing

It is numbered : 11129

© 1994 BY MÉMOIRE D'EUROPE / ÉDITIONS DE LA PORTE S.A.
ISBN 2-84150-004-7
Dépot Légal : June 1994
Printed in France in June 1994 by Oberthur Press, Rennes.
Published by MÉMOIRE D'EUROPE 41, rue du Faubourg Saint-Martin -75010 PARIS
Registered with the French Ministry of Justice on the date of publication.
Law n°49-956 of July 1949 for publications destined for the young.

ON APRIL 26, 1944, ABOVE THE PENINSULA OF COTENTIN, IN THE NEIGHBOURHOOD OF CHERBOURG, FRANCE...

SILVER LEADER TO N° 2... HEADING SOUTH... TAKE SOME FINE SNAPS FOR US, CHARLY!

PIECE OF CAKE, SILVER LEADER!

FLAK FLAK FLAKFLAK

I'VE BEEN HIT! I'M BALING OUT!

PILOT-OFFICER CHARLES LANSON IS SCREAMING...

JUMP, PHILIP! QUICK!

CHARLY! MY COCKPIT HOOD IS JAMMED! I'M FINISHED!

HOPEFULLY ONE DAY THEY'LL FIND THE PLANE'S IDENTIFICATION!

VROP... VROP...

BANG

APRIL 27, 1944, NEAR PORTSMOUTH, ENGLAND, AT SOUTHWICK HOUSE, EISENHOWER'S HEADQUARTERS ...

THE 542ⁿᵈ SQUADRON HAS TAKEN THESE PICTURES. ONE PILOT HAS DISAPPEARED DURING THE MISSION ...

IT LOOKS LIKE A GIANT UNDERGROUND CONSTRUCTION... A PLATFORM FOR DOODLEBUGS?

NO, SIR! THIS PHOTO CONFIRMS THE INFORMATION FROM THE FRENCH RESISTANCE ...

4085   106W. 133. 26·APR·44. F/36"// 542 SQDN. ←

IT'D BE A LAUNCHING PAD FOR A GIANT ROCKET!

LORD! THIS WEAPON COULD WRECK A LANDING! WE MUST BOMB IT!

SO FAR WE DON'T HAVE ANY INFORMATION ABOUT THE CONCRETE USED YET ...

THE RESISTANCE WILL PROVIDE THE INFORMATION GATHERED FROM FRENCH COMPANIES WHO'VE BUILT THE SITE FOR THE GERMANS ...

IN THE MEANTIME, IN FORMIGNY, NORMANDY, ON THE ROAD FROM BAYEUX TO CARENTAN ...

THE 352ⁿᵈ GERMAN DIVISION HAS ALMOST REACHED THE COAST, HASN'T IT?

I'VE SIGNALLED TO LONDON TWICE ...

WIE HERRLICH LEUCHTET MIR DIE NATUR.. ♫

4

THEY HAVEN'T ACKNOWLEDGED RECEPTION, HAVE THEY?

NOT AT ALL!

SEND ANOTHER PIGEON, ADRIAN!

THIS ESSENTIAL PIECE OF INFORMATION COULD MAKE THE ALLIES CHANGE THEIR LANDING PLANS...

LATER...

I'VE EVEN MENTIONED THAT THE 352nd AMOUNTS TO ABOUT 12,000 TROOPS!

A LITTLE FURTHER, ON THE ROCKY COAST, IN A GERMAN OBSERVATION POST...

HANS, A PIGEON!

THESE DAYS I KILL ONE EVERY TWO OR THREE DAYS...

PANG!

FINISHED?

NO, I STILL HAVE TO FIX THE CANTEEN.... ROMMEL IS TO ARRIVE SOON TO INSPECT THE ATLANTIC WALL...

APRIL 26, 1944, NEAR LYME BAY, ON THE SOUTH COAST OF ENGLAND...

I HOPE IT'LL BE D-DAY SOON!

GIVE HITLER A BEATING!

PASTRYCOOKS LUNCHEON AND TEA ROOMS

CAFE

GARAGE

3

I HOPE THIS ONE'S FOR REAL. I'M FED UP WITH THESE PRACTICE BOARDINGS AND LANDINGS !

RAMP -B

RAMP -A

US 370

THE WHOLE SOUTH OF THIS COUNTRY IS A VAST ENTRENCHED ENCAMPMENT FULL OF SOLDIERS AND MATERIALS,

A GIRL COULD BRING RELIEF BUT SINCE ALL LEAVE HAS BEEN SUSPENDED ...

... WE MIGHT AS WELL FIX THE KRAUTS [1] MIGHTN'T WE, SERGEANT ?

BUT OF COURSE JAMES !

(1) GERMANS

SAY, SERGEANT, DO YOU REALLY BELIEVE OUR TANKS WILL FLOAT TO THE COAST WITH THESE INFLATABLE SKIRTS ?

DURING ALL OUR MANOEUVRES OUR D. D. [2] PROVED SATISFACTORY ...

(2) DUPLEIX - DRIVE : AMPHIBIOUS TANK

SERGEANT MIKE RILEY BELONGS TO THE 743rd TANK BATTALION (1st DIVISION OF AMERICAN INFANTRY).

SO WE CAN RELY ON THEM !

PROVIDED WE DON'T LAND IN BAD WEATHER !

SERGEANT, LOTS OF MEN ARE SEASICK

HAVE THEY TAKEN PILLS ?

JAMES! ARE YOU ALL RIGHT?

HE'S DEAD!

SEND THIS MESSAGE TO THE BASE: TORPEDOED THREE BOATS IN CONVOY... SUNK TWO OF THEM.

APRIL 30, 1944.

PASTRYCOOKS LUNCHEON AND TEA ROOMS

CAFÉ

GARAGE

WELL, THEY'RE COMING BACK! SO IT WAS ONLY AN EXCERCISE!

...OR THEY WANTED TO MISLEAD HITLER!

SEVERAL HUNDREDS OF OUR BOYS HAVE DIED DURING THIS MANOEUVRE ...HOW MANY HUMAN LIVES WILL THE REAL LANDING COST?

THAT EVENING, EISENHOWER, COMMANDER-IN-CHIEF OF THE ALLIED TROOPS, EVOKES THE DRAMA WITH SIX HUNDRED CASUALTIES ALREADY

IF WE SUFFER SIMILAR ATTACKS ON D-DAY, THE WHOLE LANDING MIGHT BE JEOPARDIZED!

OUR AIR FORCE, HOWEVER, HAS CHASED AWAY THE U-BOATS(1) IN THE CHANNEL AND PREVENTED ALMOST ANY OPERATIONAL MANOEUVRE OF THE GERMAN NAVY IN THIS AREA!

(1) GERMAN SUBMARINES

"ALMOST" IS NOT GOOD ENOUGH!

OUR PILOTS ARE ALREADY DOING A GREAT JOB... THEY'LL HAVE TO DOUBLE THEIR EFFORTS!

THE NEXT DAY, AT MANSTON AIRPORT (EAST COAST OF ENGLAND)...

(1) CREW IN DANGER.

CRASH CREW (1)! BOMBER IN DIFFICULTIES APPROACHING BASE!

WELL DAN, I'LL BET YOU TEN SHILLINGS THAT IT BREAKS IN TWO AT TOUCHDOWN!

YOU'RE DISGUSTING, GORDON!

VROOAW

RATHER SAY A PRAYER FOR THOSE POOR CHAPS!

SEVERAL SQUADRONS ARE STATIONED AT MANSTON. LOCATED AT THE SEASIDE, IT IS ALSO A RESCUE AREA FOR PLANES IN DISTRESS WHEN RETURNING FROM A MISSION TO GERMANY.

CRAC

BANG

DAN KENWAY BELONGS TO THE 609th SQUADRON (11th FIGHTER GROUP R.A.F.).

MY BROTHER PHILIP DIED THIS WAY, FOUR DAYS AGO NEAR CHERBOURG ...

I KNOW, DAN! I'M SORRY!

OUR AIR-RAIDS DISORGANIZE GERMAN COMMUNICATIONS AND TRANSPORT COMPLETELY ...

A LITTLE LATER, IN THE SMALL MEETING ROOM OF THE BASE...

OUR BOMBINGS HAVE PUSHED BACK THEIR OPERATIONAL AIRSTRIPS FROM THE CHANNEL. WE CAN DO EVEN BETTER!

GERMAN AIRCRAFT IDENTIFICATION

THE PURPOSE OF THESE MISSIONS WAS BOTH TO WEAKEN THE ATLANTIC WALL DEFENSES AND TO DESTROY THE DOODLEBUG LAUNCHING PADS...

...AND PARTICULARLY TO PREVENT THEIR SUBMARINES AND PATROL BOATS FROM BURYING THEMSELVES IN THEIR BASES! IN SHORT, PREPARE OVERLORD!

FLIGHT-SERGEANT GORDON MCLAREN INTERVENES...

WHEN WILL THE FAMOUS LANDING TAKE PLACE, SIR?

GOD ONLY KNOWS, MCLAREN! DON'T BET WITH HIM!

IN THE MEANTIME, ON A BEACH IN THE SOUTH OF ENGLAND...

WHEN THE REGINA RIFLE REGIMENT LANDS IN FRANCE, THE KRAUTS WILL LOSE THEIR ARROGANCE!

FORWARD, CANADIANS!

AND HOLD YOUR RIFLES UP!

WILLIAM KEAGAN CAN HARDLY SWIM...

IF ON D-DAY THERE ARE HOLES IN THE BEACH, I'LL BE A GONER!

THE 1ST OF MAY, NEAR THE ENGLISH TOWN BEXHILL, IN THE TRAINING CAMP OF THE 1ST BATTALION OF FRENCH MARINES (INTEGRATED IN THE 4TH BRITISH COMMANDO).

FASTER, BOYS! OTHERWISE YOU'LL ALL BE DEAD ON ARRIVAL!

COME ON, LIEUTENANT, TELL US WHICH PORT HAS A PEDESTRIAN PASSAGE LIKE THIS... THEN WE'LL KNOW THE LANDING PLACE!

A BIT LATER...

THAT IS THE BEST KEPT SECRET ON EARTH, LE SAULT!

ON MAY 2ND, ERWIN ROMMEL INSPECTS A REINFORCED POINT OF THE ATLANTIC WALL...

WHAT'S HE DOING?

TALKING SHOP!

WE MUST INCREASE THE OBSTACLES AND THE MINES ON THESE BEACHES!

EVERYTHING WILL HAPPEN HERE... IF THE ENEMY CAN LAND, WE'LL LOSE THE WAR!

IN FACT, THE ENEMY'S AIRFORCE WILL DESTROY OUR REINFORCEMENTS BEFORE COMING ASHORE...

I'VE SAID IT BEFORE... THE FIRST TWENTY-FOUR HOURS OF THE INVASION WILL BE DECISIVE!

BOTH FOR THE ALLIES AND FOR US THIS WILL BE THE LONGEST DAY!

HERR MARSHAL, DOES OUR INTELLIGENCE SERVICE HAVE INFORMATION ABOUT THE INVASION?

NOTHING DEFINITE, BUT WE TEND TO THINK IT WILL HAPPEN IN THE STRAITS OF DOVER!

THE FÜHRER, ON THE OTHER HAND, FORESEES IT IN NORMANDY!

THEY'VE LEFT!

COULD WE REALLY RESIST SUCH A MASSIVE LANDING?

SURE! THAT'S WHAT THE ATLANTIC WALL IS FOR!

AND THEN WE HAVE TEN TANK DIVISIONS BEHIND US IN FRANCE, WHICH ARE READY FOR ACTION AT THE FIRST ALERT!

12. PANZER-DIVISION "HITLERJUGEND"

IN FRANCE, IN EVREUX, AT THE HEADQUARTERS OF THE 12th TANK DIVISION SS "HITLERJUGEND",...

OUR "USTUFS" [1] GO FOR DINNER AT SOLANGE'S, LIKE EVERY WEEKEND,...

I DON'T LIKE THAT PLACE! ITS CUSTOMERS LOOK LIKE TERRORISTS!

(1) UNTERSTURMFÜHRER: SUBLIEUTENANT.

G. VAN DESSEL

10

ON MAY 8, 1944, GENERAL BERNARD MONTGOMERY (COMMANDER OF THE ALLIED GROUND FORCES) RAISES AN IMPORTANT MATTER...

OUR SHOCK TROOPS HAVE REACHED THEIR POINT OF MAXIMUM PREPARATION. WE SHOULD...

...ASSIGN THE DATE OF THE INVASION, GENERAL!

OK! CONSIDERING THE NECESSARY CONDITIONS, WHICH DATES DO THE EXPERTS PROPOSE?

THERE ARE SEVERAL POSSIBILITIES... FIRST THERE ARE MAY 21, 22, 23...

MUCH TOO SOON!

JUNE 5th AND 6th WOULD BE SUITABLE ...AT THE LIMIT THE 7th, THEN THE 19th, 20th and 21st JUNE WOULD BE GOOD!

AFTER A LONG SILENCE...

AT WHAT TIME IS LOW TIDE ON THE MORNING OF JUNE 5?

AT ABOUT 6.30 A.M.

AND SUNRISE?

5.50 A.M.

JUNE 5 WILL BE D-DAY... IF THE WEATHER PERMITS, OF COURSE!

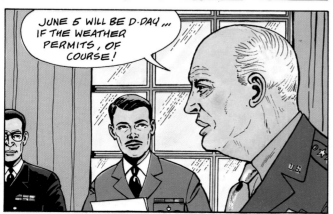

ON MAY 15, 1944, THE KING OF ENGLAND HIMSELF CHAIRS A BIG CONFERENCE...

AIR FORCE MARSHAL A.W. TEDDER, SECOND COMMANDER-IN-CHIEF, WILL REPEAT THE SCHEDULE OF OVERLORD...

THE LANDING WILL BE MADE IN NORMANDY, BETWEEN THE ORNE ESTUARY AND THE BAY OF CARENTAN ...

14

IT WILL TAKE PLACE ON FIVE BEACHES WITH AGREED NAMES... THE AMERICAN TROOPS WILL LAND ON UTAH AND OMAHA...

THE BRITISH AND CANADIAN TROOPS ON GOLD, JUNO AND SWORD...

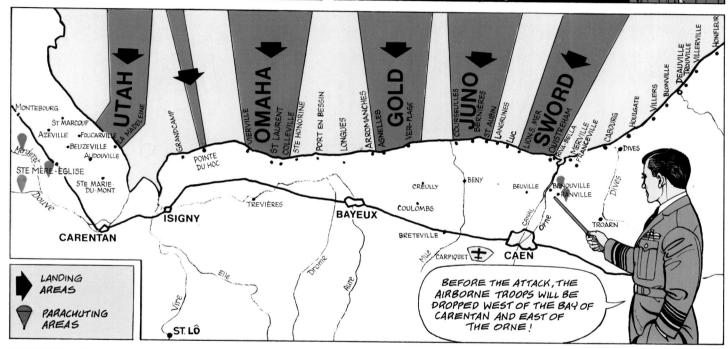

LANDING AREAS

PARACHUTING AREAS

BEFORE THE ATTACK, THE AIRBORNE TROOPS WILL BE DROPPED WEST OF THE BAY OF CARENTAN AND EAST OF THE ORNE!

AFTER THE INTERVENTIONS OF THE MILITARY, WINSTON CHURCHILL (BRITISH PRIME MINISTER) TAKES THE FLOOR...

I'VE HAD MY DOUBTS ABOUT THE SUCCESS OF OVERLORD FOR A LONG TIME, BUT NOW I'M FULLY SUPPORTING THIS PROJECT!

A SOLEMN ROYAL SPEECH ENDS THE CONFERENCE. AND A LITTLE LATER...

I'M FURIOUS AT THE IDEA THAT THE FIRST ATTACK WILL TAKE PLACE WITHOUT ME!

IT HAS TO! ROMMEL HAS TO ASSUME THAT YOUR TANKS WILL LAND IN THE STRAITS OF DOVER!

LEAVE ME PART OF THE JOB, WILL YOU?

GENERAL PATTON, CHIEF OF THE 3rd US ARMY • GENERAL BRADLEY, CHIEF OF THE 1st US ARMY

AT THE END OF MAY, THE FIRST WAVE OF TROOPS BOARD PORTS OR IMPROVISED EMBARKATION SITES.   IN TURN   THE TRANSPORT SHIPS IN HUNDREDS OF SMALL

I HOPE THIS TIME OUR PLANES AND OUR PATROLS WILL DEVASTATE THE "E-BOATS". (1)

MAY GOD HELP THEM!

THIS WRECK WILL NOT SURVIVE THE MINES!

DON'T WORRY, KEAGAN! MINESWEEPERS WILL PRECEDE THE CONVOY... OF COURSE!

HEY, LE SAULT! IF WE LAND   AT YOUR PLACE IN BRITTANY, INVITE US, WILL YOU?

(1) FAST GERMAN PATROL BOATS

AT THORNEY ISLAND...

SURPRISE, DAN! THE BIG CHIEF! IKE!

WRAAAW

I KEEP TELLING ALL THE PILOTS AT THE BASES I'M VISITING... YOU'RE FANTASTIC GUYS!

BUT SOON YOU'LL BE PUSHED TO THE LIMITS OF YOUR CAPACITIES!

D-DAY'S COMING!

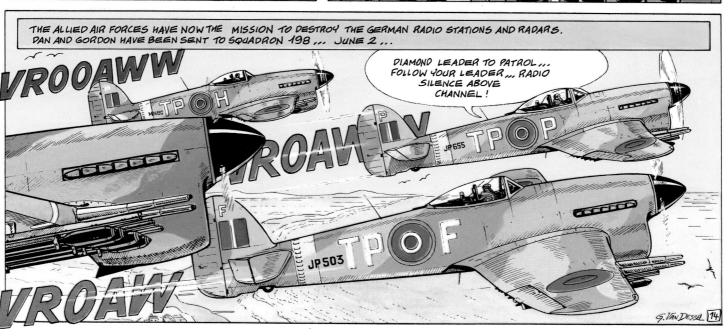

THE ALLIED AIR FORCES HAVE NOW THE MISSION TO DESTROY THE GERMAN RADIO STATIONS AND RADARS. DAN AND GORDON HAVE BEEN SENT TO SQUADRON 198... JUNE 2...

VROOAWW

DIAMOND LEADER TO PATROL... FOLLOW YOUR LEADER... RADIO SILENCE ABOVE CHANNEL!

VROAW

TP◯H MN19C

JP655 TP◯P

VROAW

JP503 TP◯F

G. VAN DESSEL 14

THE MISSION CONSISTS IN DESTROYING THE RADAR IN DIEPPE.

DIAMOND LEADER... TARGET IN SIGHT. LET'S GO!

DAN IS MUSING...

GOOD LORD! MAY I NOT END LIKE MY BROTHER PHILIP!

FROM LEADER TO Nº3: NEUTRALIZE THE "88" AT TEN O'CLOCK BELOW... ATTACK, GORDON!

O.K. DIAMOND LEADER!

BULL'S EYE!

Nº3 TO LEADER... I'VE BEEN HIT...

GET AWAY FROM HERE AND GET BACK HOME!

IN BERLIN, THE O.K.W. [1], IN THE MORNING OF JUNE 2 ...

THE GERMAN SECRET SERVICE KNEW THAT RADIO LONDON WOULD BROADCAST THE FIRST LINE OF A POEM BY VERLAINE TO SIGNAL THE IMMINENT INVASION TO THE RESISTANCE.

OUR SERVICE RECEIVED THE FIRST LINE OF VERLAINE LAST NIGHT, HERR GENERAL...

GOOD! WHAT WILL THE SECOND LINE ANNOUNCE?

[1] SUPREME HEADQUARTERS OF THE GERMAN ARMY.

AN INVASION WITHIN 48 HOURS, HERR GENERAL.

I SEE THAT ALL ARMY CORPS HAVE BEEN BROUGHT TO A STATE OF EMERGENCY! ...PERFECT!

IN FACT, INACCURACIES IN THE TRANSMISSION OF ORDERS AND THE SCEPTICISM OF CERTAIN GENERALS HAVE PREVENTED WARNING THE ARMY IN NORMANDY... AT ROMMEL'S HQ...

THIS STORY OF THE POEM IS JUST NONSENSE! THE ALLIES WON'T LAND WITH SUCH WEATHER CONDITIONS! I'M GOING TO SEIZE THE OPPORTUNITY TO LEAVE FOR GERMANY...

SUNDAY, JUNE 4, AT 4 A.M....

TEDDER, WE CANNOT LAND TOMORROW ..., D-DAY WILL BE PUT OFF TILL JUNE 6..., IF THE ANNOUNCED IMPROVEMENT IN THE WEATHER IS CONFIRMED...

GIVE THE CONVOYS THAT HAVE ALREADY SET SAIL THE ORDER TO RETURN!

OK, IKE!

ON THE MORNING OF SUNDAY, JUNE 4 ...

SIR, ALL SHIPS HAVE RETURNED EXCEPT ONE CONVOY OF 128!

DAMN IT! THEY MIGHT JEOPARDIZE OVERLORD! HAVE A FLYING BOAT. RETRIEVE THEM! HURRY UP!

SOMEWHAT LATER...

THERE! THE CONVOY! FLASH THE SIGNAL!

LOOK AT THAT FLYING BOAT, SERGEANT RILEY... IT'S ORDERING US TO RETURN!

WE'LL NEVER LAND...I DON'T BELIEVE IN IT ANY MORE!

MEANWHILE ROMMEL IS DRIVING TO GERMANY ...

AFTER MY WIFE'S BIRTHDAY PARTY, I WILL MEET THE FÜHRER ...

I'LL ASK HIM TO TRANSFER FIVE TANK DIVISIONS UNDER MY AUTHORITY AND I'LL STATION THEM ON THE COAST ...

MONDAY, JUNE 5, BY 4 A.M., IN THE LIBRARY OF SOUTHWICK HOUSE...

IF THE WEATHER DOESN'T GET ANY BETTER, OVERLORD WILL HAVE TO BE POSTPONED AGAIN!

IT'S TIME TO GO! INCIDENTALLY, THE EXPERTS FORECAST A CHANGE IN THE WEATHER FOR JUNE 6 ...

THERE IS NO CHOICE ...

WE MUST ATTACK ... WE WILL MAKE THE LANDINGS ON TUESDAY, JUNE 6 !

18

ON THE BASE AT THORNEY ISLAND, MONDAY, JUNE 5, AT NIGHTFALL...

CONTROL TO PATROL. REPEAT: YOU ARE CONFINED TO BARRACKS... IT'S FORBIDDEN TO PHONE TO THE OUTSIDE...

WE HAVE ATTACKED THE GERMAN HQ AT ST-LÔ AND BURIED ROMMEL UNDER THE BOMBS!

DAN KENWAY COULD NOT KNOW THAT ROMMEL HAD CANCELLED HIS VISIT TO ST-LÔ BECAUSE OF HIS JOURNEY TO GERMANY...

WHERE ARE YOU GOING TO WITH THIS ?

PAINT BLACK AND WHITE STRIPES ON YOUR TYPHOON, SERGEANT! WE APPLY THEM TO ALL PLANES FOR OVERLORD!

WOW! SO ALL THE CONVOYS WE SAW IN THE CHANNEL ARE THOSE OF THE INVASION! THIS TIME IT'S SERIOUS !

THE GIGANTIC INVASION MACHINE HAS COME INTO ACTION. THE AMERICAN PARATROOPERS TAKE OFF IN PLANES AND GLIDERS. IKE HAS A CHAT WITH THE TROOPS...

YOU'LL HAVE TO PAVE THE WAY FOR THE TROOPS WHO WILL LAND ON UTAH AND HOLD OUT TILL RELIEF COMES... I WANT A TOTAL VICTORY! GOOD LUCK, BOYS!

GENERAL MAXWELL TAYLOR IS IN COMMAND OF THE 101ST AMERICAN AIRBORNE DIVISION (THE SCREAMING EAGLES)

WE WILL GO FOR IT, IKE! BUT IT WON'T BE A PIECE OF CAKE!

AIRBORNE

101ST AIRBORNE

ADMIRAL BERTRAM RAMSAY (HEAD OF THE ALLIED MARINE) HAS SENT OVER 6,000 SHIPS ACROSS THE CHANNEL SO AS TO TRANSPORT OR PROTECT THE FIRST WAVE OF TROOPS...

SIR BERTRAM RAMSAY.

WHAT ARE YOU THINKING ABOUT, LE SAULT?

ABOUT TWO NUMBERS... 150,000 MEN ARE GOING TO LAND IN NORMANDY AND ONLY 177 AMONG THEM ARE FRENCH!

AIR MARSHAL SIR TRAFFORD LEIGH-MALLORY HAS ENGAGED 12,000 PLANES AND GLIDERS IN OVERLORD. INTENSIVE BOMBINGS AND DIVERSE DISTRACTION MANOEUVRES MAKE THE ENEMY BELIEVE THAT THE INVASION WILL TAKE PLACE IN THE STRAITS OF DOVER...

COMMANDER-IN-CHIEF OF THE ALLIED AIR FORCE SIR TRAFFORD LEIGH-MALLORY

CODED MESSAGES AND THE BBC BROADCASTING THE SECOND LINE [1] OF VERLAINE HAVE MOBILIZED THE RESISTANCE IN FORMIGNY ...

[1] "HURT MY HEART WITH A MONOTONOUS WEAKNESS".

ADRIEN, THEY ARE BOMBING THE COAST! THEY ARE GOING TO LAND HERE, I'M SURE!

YOU KNOW WHAT YOU'VE GOT TO DO, GASTON?

YES, I DO! WITH GUILLAUME I'M GOING TO CUT THE TELEPHONE LINES SERVING CHERBOURG AND BAYEUX...

BOUM BOUM BOUM

BE VERY CAREFUL, GASTON... THE GERMAN POLICE HAVE BEEN ABLE TO INFILTRATE OUR NETWORK ...

...AND YOU CAN'T TRUST ANYONE ABOUT HERE...

I KNOW! I MUST BE GOING ...WITH MY FIREMAN'S PASS THE GERMANS WON'T BOTHER ME !

- 1944 -

20

22

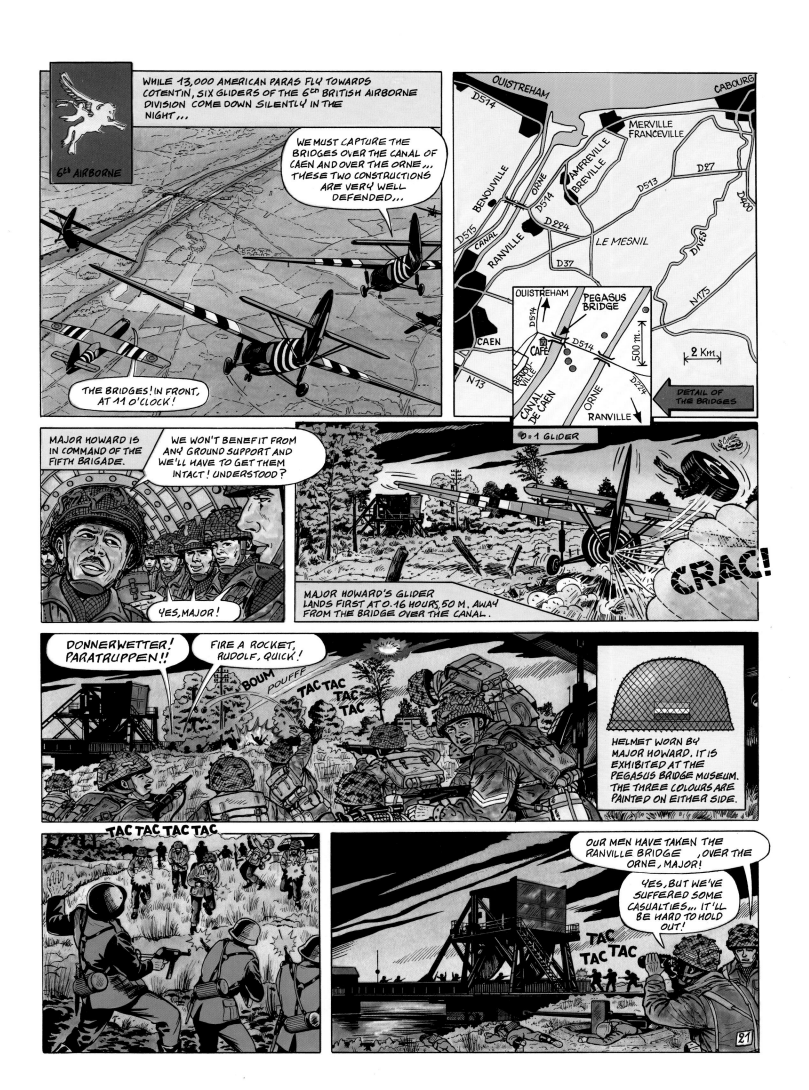

23

TAKING THESE TWO BRIDGES WAS VITAL TO ENABLE SENDING REINFORCEMENTS BY ROAD TO THE 6TH DIVISION THAT WAS GOING TO BE DROPPED BETWEEN THE ORNE AND LA DIVES.

TEN MINUTES LATER, AT 0.30 A.M., ON TUESDAY, JUNE 6, 1944 ...

... IN THE CAFÉ AT THE BRIDGE OVER THE CANAL ...

STRANGE! THE GERMANS SHOUTED "PARAS", THEY FIRED AND THEN NOTHING AT ALL !

THEY KILLED THEM ... THE POOR CHAPS!

SOLDIERS ARE COMING NEAR ... THEY LOOK LIKE NEGROES!

WHAT DOES THAT MEAN?

ANY GERMANS IN THE HOUSE?

NO! YOU CAN CHECK IT ... COME IN!

LATER ...

MADAM, WE'VE COME TO LIBERATE FRANCE ... GO TO THE BASEMENT. HEAVY FIGHTING WILL BEGIN SOON !

25

GENERAL RICHARD GALE

GENERAL GALE IS IN COMMAND OF THE 6th DIVISION, WHICH WILL HAVE TO "HOLD" THE EAST SIDE OF THE INVASION.

HOW ARE THE MEN?

MANY INJURED IN CERTAIN BRIGADES, GENERAL, AND THE WIND HAS DRIFTED THE GLIDERS VERY FAR OFF...

THE SIXTH WILL ALSO HAVE TO CONQUER THE HEIGHTS NORTHEAST OF CAEN AND DESTROY THE BRIDGES OVER LA DIVES (TO STYMIE GERMAN REINFORCEMENTS).

...BUT WE HAVE NEARLY ALL THE MATERIAL, GENERAL; THE ANTI-TANK GUNS, THE JEEPS, THE BULLDOZERS...

WELL, SEND A BATTALION TO REINFORCE MAJOR HOWARD'S POSITIONS AND ANOTHER ONE TO PROTECT RANVILLE.

MEANWHILE, NEAR COTENTIN, THE TWO U.S. AIRBORNE DIVISIONS WERE PARACHUTED VERY IMPRECISELY... AND...

TAC TAC TAC TAC TAC TAC

FIRE!

THE PARAS PROCEED AT RANDOM, ANXIOUS AND STRAINED...

LISTEN TO THESE FOOTSTEPS... I'LL USE THE GRASSHOPPER THEY GAVE US...

IF IT'S OUR MEN THEY'LL ANSWER WITH A CLICK-CLACK WITH THIS DEVICE!

STOP!

NO, BILLY! IF IT'S KRAUTS, THIS GADGET WILL GIVE US AWAY!

24

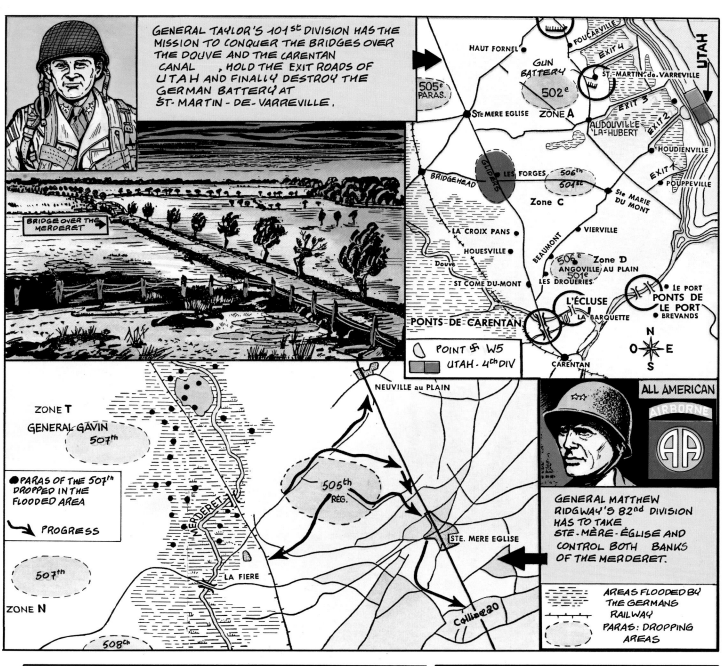

THE COMMANDOS DROPPED IN BRITTANY NOT INCLUDED, 18,000 MEN HAVE LANDED IN NORMANDY. SUCH AN IMPRESSIVE AIRBORNE OPERATION DOES NOT PASS UNNOTICED. THE GERMAN STAFF IS ALARMED ...

NEAR PARIS, IN ST-GERMAIN-EN-LAYE, MARSHAL GERD VON RUNDSTEDT, COMMANDER-IN-CHIEF OF THE WESTERN ARMIES, HAS BEEN WOKEN ...

ALL OUR INFORMATION SOURCES REPORT IMPORTANT DROPPINGS EAST OF THE ORNE AND NORTHWEST OF CARENTAN...

IT'S THE ANNOUNCEMENT OF A GREAT OFFENSIVE IN NORMANDY, HERR MARSHALL!

DIVERSIONARY TACTIC, BLUMENTRITT! THE REAL INVASION WILL HAPPEN IN THE STRAITS OF DOVER...

GUNTHER BLUMENTRITT, CHIEF-OF-STAFF OF VON RUNDSTEDT.

BUT VON RUNDSTEDT REACTS...

I WON'T TAKE ANY RISK... I'LL SEND TWO SPARE TANK DIVISIONS TO THE COAST...

THE FÜHRER MUST AUTHORIZE THAT, HERR MARSHAL!

WELL THEN, ASK THE O.K.W.!

VON RUNDSTEDT'S HQ IN ST-GERMAIN-EN-LAYE

GENERAL ALFRED JODL DIRECTS THE OPERATIONS OFFICE AT THE O.K.W.

YOUR INFORMATION IS CONFUSED AND CONTRADICTORY, BLUMENTRITT... IT'S NOT IMPORTANT ENOUGH TO WAKE THE FÜHRER... WE'LL TALK TO HIM ABOUT THAT IN THE MORNING!

GENTLEMEN, JODL REFUSES TO WAKE THE FÜHRER ...SEE YOU LATER!

?!

DONNERWETTER!

CLAC

HE HE! IT'S HOT IN NORMANDY BUT THE FÜHRER'S SOUND ASLEEP!

!

HA HA HAHA!

SOLDAT SCHÖRNER, MAKE US SOME COFFEE INSTEAD OF LAUGHING LIKE A CLOWN!

86

AROUND 4.30 A.M. LT.-COLONEL OTWAY'S MEN TAKE THE BATTERY AT MERVILLE.

TAC TAC TAC

AAAH!

TAC TA

AFTER A WILD BATTLE...

WE'VE DESTROYED THE GUNS OF THIS DAMNED BATTERY AND FIRED THE YELLOW ROCKET TO SIGNAL THE SUCCESS OF OUR MISSION TO THE CRUISER "ARETHUSA"...

SEND A CONFIRMATION BY PIGEON!

MEANWHILE THE 101st DIVISION TOOK NEARLY ALL UTAH EXIT ROADS, AND PARAS OF THE 82nd FREED STE-MÈRE-ÉGLISE...

AT 5 A.M. THE GREATEST ARMADA OF ALL TIMES COMES WITHIN SIGHT OF THE FRENCH COAST...

MESSAGE FROM GENERAL GALE: THE 6th DIVISION HAS SUFFERED LOSSES BUT HAS ACHIEVED ITS GOAL.

IN CHERBOURG, AT THE LISTENING POST OF THE KRIEGSMARINE(1)...

OUR SOUND DETECTORS SIGNAL SHIP NOISES IN THE BAY OF THE SEINE, ADMIRAL!

TRY TO WARN THE GENERAL STAFF ONCE MORE!

IT'S MOST DIFFICULT! WE'VE NO TELEPHONE AND THE ENEMY'S RAIDS HAVE DAMAGED OUR RADIO TRANSMITTERS...

(1) GERMAN WAR MARINE

SUDDENLY, THREE E-BOATS COMING FROM LE HAVRE, EMERGE FROM THE ARTIFICIAL FOG HEADING FOR THE ARMADA...

FIRE!

ALL OUR BIG CHIEFS HAVE BEEN WRONG... THE INVASION WILL HAPPEN IN NORMANDY!

ON BOARD SIR RAMSAY'S FLAGSHIP...

BY MIRACLE ONLY ONE SHIP HAS BEEN SUNK, SIR...

DOUBLE THE LOOK-OUTS AND GET THE BIG GUNS READY...

27

SUDDENLY AN "88" FIRES ...

BANG!

WE'RE LUCKY! A SHELL HAS CLEARED THE WAY!

DON'T STAY THERE! FORWARD!

SHORTLY AFTER 7 A.M. THE 2ND RANGER BATTALION ATTACKS LA POINTE DU HOC, FROM WHERE A POWERFUL BATTERY MENACES OMAHA ...

2ND RANGER BN

BAOUM

IN SPITE OF SEVERE LOSSES, A HANDFUL OF RANGERS REACHES THE TOP OF THE CLIFF ...

BANG

TAC TAC TAC

TAC TAC TAC TAC

THE BATTERY'S OVER THERE!

TAC TAC TAC TAC

MEANWHILE, IN LILLE, WING COMMANDER JOSEPH PRILLER ANSWERS THE PHONE ...

THEY HAVE LANDED? ... AND YOU WANT ME TO HURRY? IS THAT A JOKE? YOU'VE ONLY LEFT ME TWO PLANES !!!

OBEY THE ORDERS, PRILLER!

30

32

A LITTLE BEFORE 8 A.M., THE CANADIANS LAND AT JUNO (FROM GRAYE-SUR-MER TO ST.-AUBIN).

BOM

LCA210

BAM

LORD! ANOTHER WARCRAFT BLOWN...THE HIGH TIDE PREVENTS THEM SEEING THE MINES...

... AND THE SWELL MAKES THE LANDING BARGES CAPSIZE!

A1126

HOLD ON TO ME, WILLIE!

HELP!

BOUM

FEUER!

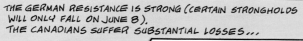
THE GERMAN RESISTANCE IS STRONG (CERTAIN STRONGHOLDS WILL ONLY FALL ON JUNE 8).
THE CANADIANS SUFFER SUBSTANTIAL LOSSES...

FORWARD! LONG LIVE THE REGINA!

MEANWHILE, THE FRENCH MARINES ARE PROCEEDING UNDER HEAVY FIRE IN OUISTREHAM AND ATTACKING THE CASINO...

TAC TAC TAC

TAC TAC TAC

1st B'ION F.M. COMMANDO

SHOTS ARE ALSO COMING FROM THE CASINO'S BASEMENT...

TAC TAC TAC

BOUM

BOM

COMMANDED BY PHILIPPE KIEFFER, THE FRENCH MARINES TAKE THE BUILDING BY STORM...

BAM

AT 9.33 A.M. GENERAL EISENHOWER HAS THE WHOLE WORLD INFORMED ABOUT THE LANDINGS AT LA ROCHE GUYON (NEAR PARIS) AT ROMMELS HQ...

HERR GENERAL, I'VE GOT A COMPLETE REPORT ON THE INVASION... THE OFFENSIVE APPEARS TO BE VERY IMPORTANT!

GENERAL HANS SPEIDEL IS MARSHAL ROMMEL'S CHIEF-OF-STAFF...

INDEED, IT'S A MASSIVE OPERATION! I WILL PHONE THE MARSHAL!

...THE INVADER IS ONLY SMALL FRY THAT WE WILL THROW BACK IN THE SEA! GET READY, GENTLEMEN!

IN EVREUX, KURT MEYER (A "H.TLER JUGEND" CHIEF) HAS ASSEMBLED HIS OFFICERS...

GENTLEMEN, "THEY" HAVE LANDED, BUT WE HAVEN'T HAD THE ORDER TO ATTACK YET,,,

BY THE END OF THE MORNING, IN FORMIGNY (5 KM AWAY FROM THE OMAHA AREA), ON THE ROOF OF ADRIEN'S FARM...

STRAIN YOUR EYES, GASTON! WHAT DO YOU SEE?

NOTHING! THEY MUST STILL BE ON THE BEACH...

BLAM

NO! A TANK IS COMING ON THE COASTAL ROAD... IT'S FIRING!

ON BOARD A DESTROYER...

THANKS TO THIS SHOOTING I CAN LOCATE THE BATTERY THAT IS SLAUGHTERING OUR BOYS! COME A BIT CLOSER TO THE BEACH!

33

WE'RE TAKING RISKS, COMMANDER!

IT'S OUR SOLDIERS WHO ARE TAKING RISKS! BLOW UP THAT BATTERY!

SUPPORTED BY A CRUISER, THE DESTROYER CRUSHES THE MOULINS BATTERY WITH MORTAR-SHELLS!

THE KRAUTS ARE SURRENDERING! FINALLY THE ROAD IS OPEN! FORWARD!

ERNEST HEMINGWAY IS PONDERING OVER THE ARTICLE HE WILL WRITE FOR "COLLIER'S"...

IN SMALL GROUPS OUR SORELY TRIED SOLDIERS ARE LEAVING THE BEACH.

IN FRONT OF US THERE IS A GREEN LANDSCAPE... I SEE BEAUTIFUL MEADOWS, A SHELLED VILLAGE, BUT NO ENEMY! AND YET, THE DEAD LAY LITTERED ON THE BEACH...

I HAVE THE IMPRESSION OF HAVING DREAMT THE BLOODY OMAHA NIGHTMARE!

AT NOON, IN FRONT OF THE ENGLISH HOUSE OF COMMONS, CHURCHILL CONFIRMS THE ALLIES' CAPTURE OF ROME AND THEN DESCRIBES THE INVASION IN STYLE ...

AT SEA AND BY AIR, THOUSANDS OF LINES DRAW THE WORLD OF FREEDOM ...

AT 1.30 P.M. AT THE BÉNOUVILLE BRIDGE WHERE MAJOR HOWARD HAS PUSHED BACK SEVERAL GERMAN COUNTERATTACKS...

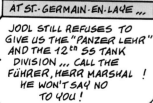

AT ST.-GERMAIN-EN-LAYE...

JODL STILL REFUSES TO GIVE US THE "PANZER LEHR" AND THE 12th SS TANK DIVISION ... CALL THE FÜHRER, HERR MARSHAL! HE WON'T SAY NO TO YOU!

NO, I WON'T BEG THE FÜHRER, BLUMENTRITT ...

BOUM

BOUM

I'M FED UP WITH BEING UNDER FIRE WITHOUT REACTING ... AND COMMANDO 4 HASN'T ARRIVED YET!

34

A LITTLE LATER...

ROGER!

FROM BLUE 1 TO BLUE 2...
ARMOURED CONVOY AT TWO O'CLOCK...
LEAD THE WAY, KENWAY!
GO!

PASS AUF! TIEFFLIEGER!(1)

ZOUF

(1) ATTENTION! NOSE DIVE ATTACK

TAC TAC TAC

TEUFEL! WHERE ARE OUR PLANES?

IN THE MEANTIME, ANOTHER TANK DIVISION, THE 21st PANZER, HAS BEEN ORDERED TO ATTACK IN THE DIRECTION OF SWORD. ITS TANKS ARE CROSSING CAEN...

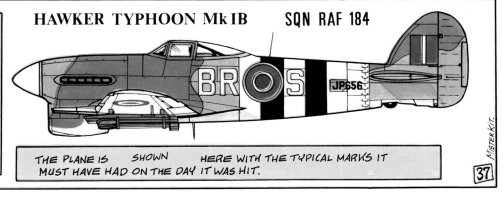

HAWKER TYPHOON Mk IB   SQN RAF 184

THE CAEN MEMORIAL DISPLAYS IN ITS HALL A BEAUTIFUL LIFE-SIZE REPLICA OF A "ROCKET TYPHOON". THIS MACHINE WAS HIT BY THE FLAK ON JUNE 7, 1944, WHEN IT ATTACKED A RAILWAY CONVOY IN THE STATION OF MEZIDON. (RAILWAY LINE CAEN-PARIS). THE PILOT, FLIGHT SGT. J.J. ROWLAND, WAS KILLED.

BROS   JP656

MISTER KIT.

THE PLANE IS SHOWN HERE WITH THE TYPICAL MARKS IT MUST HAVE HAD ON THE DAY IT WAS HIT.

37

ONE UNIT SUCCEEDS IN PENETRATING AUDACIOUSLY AS FAR AS LUC-SUR-MER...

MEIN GOTT! IT'S INCREDIBLE!

THEY REALLY HAVE LANDED!

ATTENTION! ENEMY TANKS ON YOUR EAST FLANK!

GET BACK! HIDE IN THE UNDERGROWTH!

FEUER!

LATER, AT SUNSET...

THEY'R DROPPING GLIDERS BEHIND US! GENERAL WITHDRAWAL TO CAEN!

THE GERMANS COULD NOT KNOW THAT THESE LATEST REINFORCEMENTS WERE INTENDED FOR GENERAL GALE'S 6th DIVISION...

HEY, DON'T LEAVE, OR WE'RE DONE FOR! MY DIVISION HAS SUFFERED SEVERE LOSSES!

WE CAN'T DO ANYTHING FOR YOU, HERR GENERAL!

WE'RE GOING TO BE SURROUNDED AND WE DON'T HAVE ANY SUPPORT!

YOU BASTARDS! THAT'S HOW YOU LOSE A WAR!

AT LA ROCHE-GUYON, WHERE MARSHAL ROMMEL HAS RETURNED AT THE END OF THE DAY...

I SHOULD HAVE KNOWN THEY'D LAND IN NORMANDY!

THE 21st PANZER'S COUNTER-ATTACK HAS FAILED, HERR MARSHAL ...WILL WE BE ABLE TO PUSH BACK THE ENEMY?

I HOPE SO! I'VE ALWAYS WON MY BATTLES... BUT FOR NOW I'M EXHAUSTED! IT'S BEEN A VERY, VERY LONG DAY, SPEIDEL!

40

AT NIGHT, THE WAR CORRESPONDENTS TAKE THE OPPORTUNITY TO FINISH THEIR COVERAGE...

THAT MADMAN WITH THE TYPEWRITER WILL GIVE US AWAY!

HE'S JUMPED WITH IT. WHY SHOULDN'T HE USE IT NOW?

... I AM WITH THE 82nd AIRBORNE DIVISION SOMEWHERE IN NORMANDY, IN A RUINED FARM...

OUTSIDE, THE GENERAL IS ENCOURAGING THE MEN... WE HAVE SUFFERED SEVERE LOSSES AND WE WILL HAVE TO MAKE IT THROUGH THE NIGHT, IN SPITE OF THE EXHAUSTION ...

ON THE GERMAN SIDE, AT THE COMMAND POST OF THE 726th INFANTRY REGIMENT, NEAR COLLEVILLE[1]...

NEXT TO ME IS A HERO... HIS NAME IS HEIN SEVERLOH... HE IS 21... WITH HIS MACHINE GUN, IN THE VIERVILLE AREA[1]...

... HE FIRED OVER 12,000 CARTRIDGES AT THE ENEMY CONTINUOUSLY FROM 6.30 A.M. TILL NOON... THOUGH INJURED HE HAS BEEN ABLE TO WITHDRAW TO THIS PLACE...

CLOSE TO COLLEVILLE...

WE'RE HOLDING ON TIGHT TO THE COAST... IF THE KRAUTS ATTACK TOMORROW, THEY'LL THROW US BACK!

NOT SURE! THEY HAVE BEEN TAKEN BY SURPRISE! LET'S HOPE THE LANDING WILL SUCCEED!

[1] AREA OF OMAHA

MEANWHILE THE RANGERS AT LA POINTE DU HOC HAVE TAKEN THE BATTERY, BUT DURING THE NIGHT THE GERMANS ARE COUNTERATTACKING...

ERGEBT EUCH![2] YOU'RE SURROUNDED!

SHOW YOURSELF!

PANG PANG TAC TAC TAC TAC TAC PANG

[2] SURRENDER!

COLONEL RUDDER COMMANDS THE RANGER BATTALION...

WE'RE RUNNING OUT OF AMMUNITION... IT WON'T BE EASY TO KEEP OUR POSITION UNTIL THE REINFORCEMENTS GET HERE...

WE'LL HOLD OUT!

RANGERS

39

Deutsche A

Berlin, Mittwoch, 7. Juni 1944

BOOTH'S DRY GIN

News Chronicle
4 a.m. EDITION

SKIN TROUBLE

'ŒUVRI

DERNIÈRE ÉDITION — 5 H. DU MATIN — UN FRANC

WE HOLD THREE BRIDGEHEADS

Allies battling inland: paratroops astride key road: tanks driving on Caen: Nazis expect new landings

Die Invasion hat begonnen

l'Unita

roupes anglo-américaines

ont débarqué hier par mer et par la voie des airs

entre Cherbourg et Le Havre

5H. Le Nouvelliste

MERCREDI 7 JUIN 1944 — UN Franc

Proletari di tutti i paesi, unitevi!

IL SECONDO FRONTE E' IN ATTO, ROMA E' LIBERATA:

AVANTI PER L'INSURREZIONE NAZIONALE!

nolls Times

TUESDAY MORNING, JUNE 6, 1944

LES ANGLO-AMÉRICAINS OPÈRENT
un débarquement sur la côte normande

NAZIS SAY INVASION ON

IN SAINT-LÔ, AT THE COMMAND POST OF THE 84th GERMAN CORPS...

COMMANDER, YOU'RE SPEAKING WITH OUR CORRESPONDENT AT BAYEUX, FRAULEIN KATRIN...

HELLO?

COMMANDER, I MUST INFORM YOU THAT THE ENGLISH TANKS ARE PARADING IN THE STREETS... BAYEUX HAS FALLEN!

IS THAT A JOKE, KATRIN?

NOT AT ALL! LISTEN...

LONG LIVE THE ALLIES! VICTORY! HURRAY!

AND WHAT WILL BECOME OF YOU?

I'LL MANAGE QUITE WELL...

... BECAUSE THE MEN HAVE LEFT ME!

AT POINTE DU HOC, WHERE COLONEL RUDDER RESISTS THE GERMAN ATTACKS WITH LESS THAN A HUNRED RANGERS... HE HAS BEEN INJURED...

SEND A SIGNAL TO THE VESSELS OUT ON THE HIGH SEA...

...THEIR GUNS MUST COVER OUR POSITION OR WE'LL BE OVERRUN BY THE ENEMY ...

COLONEL RUDDER AND HIS MEN WILL ONLY BE RELIEVED ON JUNE 8, AT DAYBREAK...

40

IN ARDENNE ABBEY... (5 KM. FROM CAEN), RESIDENCE OF K. MEYER...

WHAT HAVE YOU BEEN DOING, KERNER? I'VE BEEN WAITING FOR YOU ALL NIGHT!

THE JABOS[1] ARE ATTACKING ALL CONVOYS AND WE HAD TO DRIVE AT NIGHT AFTER HAVING HIDDEN FOR HOURS UNDER THE APPLETREES!

[1] ALLIED FIGHTERS

ALL RIGHT! THIS ABBEY WILL BECOME MY COMMAND POST... YOU'LL ENSURE ITS DEFENCE!

WITHIN A COUPLE OF HOURS WE'LL BURST THROUGH THE ALLIED FRONT. ROMMEL'S ORDERS!

MEANWHILE, THE REGINA RIFLE REGIMENT HAS FREED THE VILLAGES OF BRETTEVILLE AND NORREY (10 KM. NW OF CAEN).

BE CAREFUL! HERE SS TANK UNITS ARE READY TO ATTACK...

THANKS FOR THE WARNING... WE'LL TAKE UP A DEFENSIVE POSITION IN THE AREA.

PATROL THE NEIGHBOURHOOD THOROUGHLY IN THE DIRECTION OF CAEN!

LT.-COLONEL FOSTER "MATT" MATHESON IN COMMAND OF THE "REGINA"...

IN THE AFTERNOON, A SMALL RECONNAISSANCE GROUP COMES ACROSS A "HITLERJUGEND" UNIT...

FEUER!

PANG! TAC TAC TAC TAC

WILLIAM KEAGAN AND TERRANCE FLEE LIKE HUNTED ANIMALS...

THEY'VE HIT JIMMY!

LET'S GET AWAY FROM HERE!

KOT KOOT!

LATER...

WE'RE LOST, WILLIE!

STILL, WE'RE ALIVE... LET'S HEAD NORTH!

41

JUNE 7, AT THE END OF THE DAY, TYPHOONS ARE HUNTING GERMAN TANKS SOUTH OF CAEN. SGT. KENWAY IS FLYING WITH HIS FORMATION...

ZOUF

FROM RED LEADER... ATTENTION! THE FLAK IS ACCURATE!

FROM N° 3 TO RED LEADER, THE FUSELAGE HAS BEEN HIT BY "37"'S AND...

CROOOW CROOOW...

RADIO BREAKDOWN!

I MUST LAND SOMEWHERE... I'M TOO LOW TO BAILOUT!

VROP... VROP...

NEAR BY, IN THE RANVILLE AREA...

HOLD ON TIGHT! WE'RE COMING!

DAMN!... WHERE DID THAT PLANE COME FROM?

⁉

PHEW!

GOOD LORD! THAT WAS A NARROW SHAVE

BANG CRAC!

43

WHEN I ENTERED BRETEVILLE I MISSED AN SS ON A MOTORCYCLE...

...IT'S THE ONE WHO ORDERED THE SLAUGHTERING OF OUR PRISONERS! BUT I'LL FIND HIM!

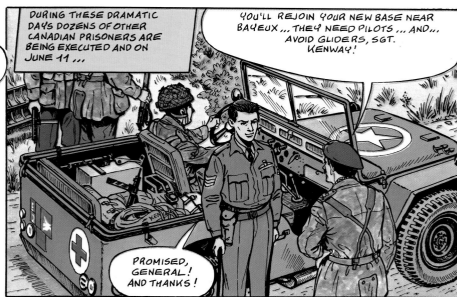

DURING THESE DRAMATIC DAYS DOZENS OF OTHER CANADIAN PRISONERS ARE BEING EXECUTED AND ON JUNE 11...

YOU'LL REJOIN YOUR NEW BASE NEAR BAYEUX... THEY NEED PILOTS... AND... AVOID GLIDERS, SGT. KENWAY!

PROMISED, GENERAL! AND THANKS!

IS... IS THE ROAD SAFE?

ALL BRIDGEHEAD LINKS UP TO AND INCLUDING OMAHA HAVE BEEN ENSURED AND ALL RESISTANCE POCKETS HAVE BEEN OVERCOME!

THE BELGIAN COLONEL RAYMOND LALLEMANT (NICKNAMED "HORSE") WELCOMES DAN ON BEHALF OF SQUADRON 609...

WELCOME, SGT. KENWAY, TO BASE B7! COMMANDOES ARE RELOADING OUR PLANES AND OFF WE GO!

IS THAT THE AIRFIELD? WE HAVE TO MOVE THE COWS TO TAKE OFF?

IT'S NOT AN AIRFIELD BUT A FAKE TARGET FOR THE GERMAN MORTARS!

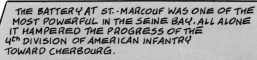

THE BATTERY AT ST.-MARCOUF WAS ONE OF THE MOST POWERFUL IN THE SEINE BAY. ALL ALONE IT HAMPERED THE PROGRESS OF THE 4TH DIVISION OF AMERICAN INFANTRY TOWARD CHERBOURG.

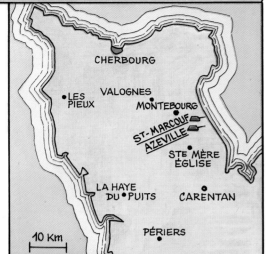

CHERBOURG

VALOGNES
• LES PIEUX
MONTEBOURG •
ST-MARCOUF
AZEVILLE
STE MÈRE ÉGLISE

LA HAYE DU • PUITS   CARENTAN •

PÉRIERS

10 Km

THE BASE HAS BEEN SURROUNDED SINCE JUNE 7...

THE KRAUTS IN THERE HAVE 600 TONS OF BOMBS AND THE DAY BEFORE YESTERDAY THEY WERE STILL SHOOTING AT UTAH...

THEY HAVE EVEN BEEN SHOT BY THEIR BATTERY AT AZEVILLE TO DRIVE US BACK!

THAT JUNE 11, IN THE CENTRAL BUNKER...

LIEUTENANT OHMSEN... I'M LISTENING!

THIS IS ADMIRAL HENNECKE AT CHERBOURG... HOW MANY MEN HAVE YOU LEFT, OHMSEN?

ABOUT 80, WITHOUT THE SERIOUSLY INJURED...

TRY TO GET AWAY! OUR POSITIONS ARE ONLY 10 KM. AWAY!

BURN ALL THE SECRET DOCUMENTS... TONIGHT WE'LL BE SNEAKING THROUGH THE ENEMY'S LINES...

AT THE END OF THE DAY, AT CARENTAN, SOUTH OF THE CITY...

BOULANGERIE

HEIL HITLER! MY SS DIVISION IS COMING TO REINFORCE YOUR PARAS... WHERE IS THE AMERICAN ADVANCE GUARD, HERR COLONEL?

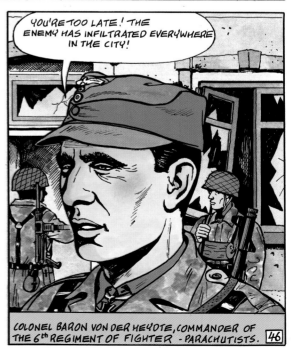

YOU'RE TOO LATE! THE ENEMY HAS INFILTRATED EVERYWHERE IN THE CITY!

COLONEL BARON VON DER HEYOTE, COMMANDER OF THE 6TH REGIMENT OF FIGHTER-PARACHUTISTS. 46

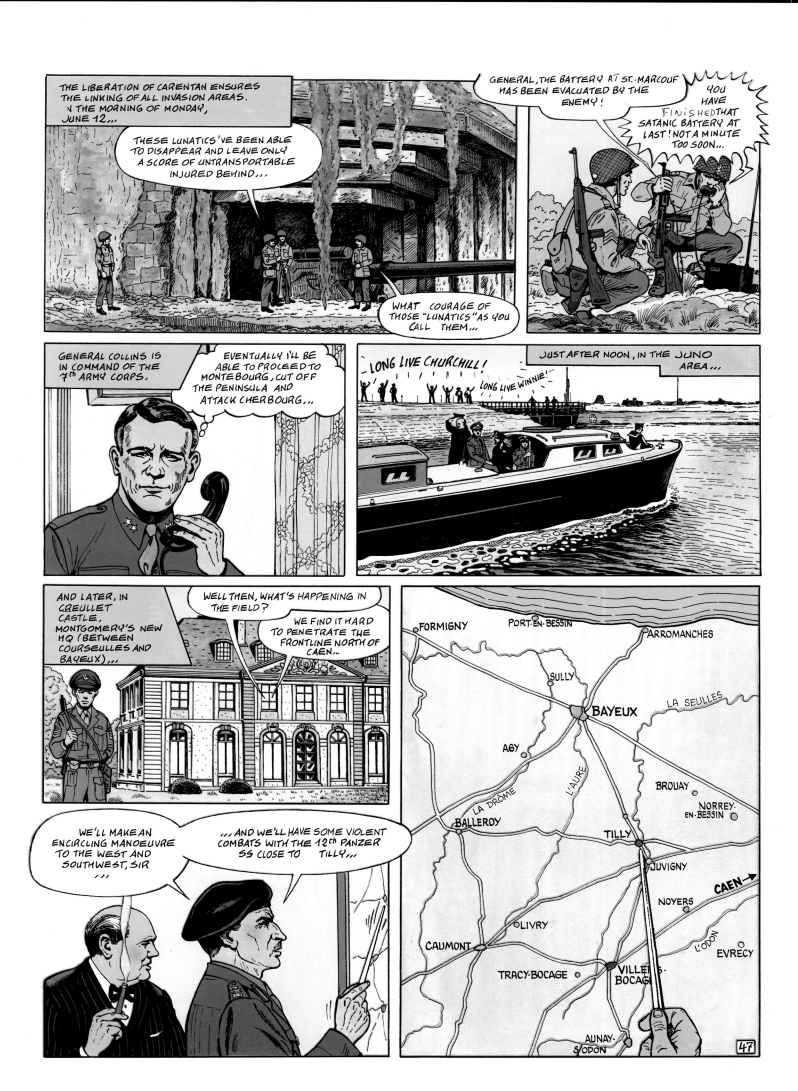

49

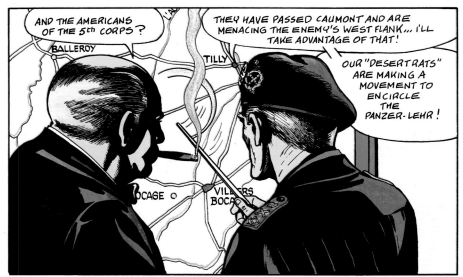

AND THE AMERICANS OF THE 5TH CORPS?

THEY HAVE PASSED CAUMONT AND ARE MENACING THE ENEMY'S WEST FLANK... I'LL TAKE ADVANTAGE OF THAT!

OUR "DESERT RATS" ARE MAKING A MOVEMENT TO ENCIRCLE THE PANZER-LEHR!

"MONTY"'S BERET

AMONG ITS REMARKABLE COLLECTION OF UNIFORMS BAYEUX' MEMORIAL MUSEUM OF THE BATTLE OF NORMANDY DISPLAYS MARSHAL MONTGOMERY'S AUTHENTIC AND FAMOUS BLACK BERET.

INDEED 300 TANKS OF THE 7TH BRITISH DIVISION (THE FAMOUS "DESERT RATS") ARE PROCEEDING TOWARD VILLERS-BOCAGE...

"THE DESERT RATS"

MEANWHILE SGT. RILEY IS WITH THE 5TH AMERICAN CORPS IN THE CAUMONT AREA...

DO YOU KNOW CHEWING GUM? HERE!

TASTE OUR CIDER! IT'S THE DRINK OF THE NORMANS...

THAT'LL DO! START THE ENGINES... LET'S GO!

VROM

IN ST. GERMAIN-EN-LAYE, AT VON RUNDSTEDT'S H.Q. ...

BAD NEWS, HERR MARSHAL ..."THE COMMANDER OF THE 64TH ARMY CORPS GOT KILLED NEAR ST-LÔ ,,,

GENERAL ERICH MARCKS IS DEAD?

AN ATTACK BY THE "JABOS" DID HIM IN, HERR MARSHAL!

HE WAS A GREAT SOLDIER, BLUMENTRITT, A FINE MAN AND A FRIEND ,,,

48

50

AROUND 8.30 A.M. ON TUESDAY, JUNE 13, AT THE EASTERN EXIT OF VILLERS-BOCAGE...

YES, YES... MY EARS HAVEN'T FOOLED ME! THE "DESERT RATS" INDEED!

OBERSTURMFÜHRER[1] MICHAEL WITTMANN HAS DESTROYED 117 OF THE ENEMY'S TANKS IN RUSSIA. HIS 57-TON "TIGER" BOUNCES...

RANGE 70 M. ... ANTI-TANK SHELL! ASK FOR REINFORCEMENTS ...

VROAW

[1] LIEUTENANT

WITTMANN HEADS FOR A COLUMN OF BRITISH "CROMWELLS" AND PROVOKES A DISASTER ...

1st SS PZ. CPS. BADGE

WHAM

BAM BAM BAM

A DOZEN "TIGERS" ARE COMING TO JOIN US, HERR OSTUF! [1]

[1] ABBREVIATION FOR "OBERSTURMFÜHRER".

A STREET FIGHT LENGTHENS THE "TIGER" TANK-ATTACK, THE ENGLISH ATTEMPT TO BREAK THROUGH HAS FAILED AND VILLERS-BOCAGE FALLS BACK INTO THE HANDS OF THE PANZER-LEHR...

PANZER-LEHR DIVISION

TAC-TAC-TAC

MEANWHILE...

WELL, DAN, YOU'RE OK?

NO! THE DUST, THE NOISE NIGHT AND DAY, THE GERMAN SHELLS, I'M FED UP WITH IT!

LET'S NOT COMPLAIN TOO MUCH ... FLYING BOMBS[1] ARE FALLING ON LONDON!

[1] THE V1'S

49

THAT NIGHT, LIKE THE PREVIOUS NIGHTS, AT THE BRIDGEHEAD OF THE ORNE, NEAR AMFREVILLE ...

I CAN'T GO ON! NOT A SINGLE MOMENT OF REST FOR A WEEK NOW... AND ONLY DEFENSIVE COMBATS ...

...AND THEY'RE LETHAL! WE SEEM TO HAVE LOST HALF OUR MEN SINCE THE LANDING ...

ARE YOU SURPRISED? ON THE OTHER SIDE THEY ARE FIVE OR SIX TIMES AS MANY... HEY! LOOK AT THAT... BUT...

BUT...

BUT THAT'S ONE OF US!

DON'T GO LE SAULT!

WE CAN'T LEAVE HIM THERE!

PANG TAC TAC TAC

COVER ME!

PIOUWW PIOUWW PIOUWW PIOUWWW

IT'S LIEUTENANT LONGREEN! HE'S STILL ALIVE... WE MUST EVACUATE HIM!...

TAC TAC TAC PANG PANG

THE LIEUTENANT HAD BEEN INJURED WHEN RETURNING FROM A MISSION BEHIND THE ENEMY'S LINES, IT WILL TAKE A DAY TO BRING HIM BACK!

TAC TACTAC TAC

CLAC

TAC TAC TAC

BADGES WORN ON THE SLEEVES BY THE FRENCH COMMANDOS OF COMMANDER KIEFFER.

FRANCE

N°4 COMMANDO

THE FOURTH COMMANDO MUSEUM AT OUISTREHAM EXHIBITS NUMEROUS PERSONAL SOUVENIRS OF FRENCH COMMANDOS, AS WELL AS VERY DIVERSE MATERIAL OF BOTH ALLIES AND GERMANS.

ON JUNE 14, GENERAL DE GAULLE LANDS IN THE JUNO AREA AND GOES TO BAYEUX WHERE HE IS BEING WELCOMED ENTHUSIASTICALLY.

VROM

M5537365

50

ON JUNE 16, MONTGOMERY WELCOMES THE KING OF ENGLAND, GEORGE VI, AT HIS HQ IN CREULLET. ON MONDAY, JUNE 19, TILLY IS TAKEN.

DAMNED! THE CITY DOES NOT EXIST ANYMORE!

NORMAL! IT HAD TO TAKE OVER 30,000 SHELLS!

MINE CLEARING CONTINUES... AN ENGINEER PLACES A WARNING SIGN THAT THE SIDES OF THE ROAD ARE MINED.

MINES IN VERGES

IN ST.-GERMAIN-EN-LAYE, AT VON RUNDSTEDT'S HQ...

WE'LL BLOCK THE ENEMY SOUTH OF TILLY AND CAUMONT, BUT THE AMERICANS ARE MOVING TO CHERBOURG WITH THREE DIVISIONS...

IF WE COULD FIRE V1'S ONTO THE LANDING BEACHES, THAT WOULD HELP US A LOT!

I SUGGESTED THAT TO THE FÜHRER..., BUT HE OVERRULED ME! HE WANTS TO DESTROY LONDON!

AND THE REINFORCEMENTS?

ARROMANCHES

BAYEUX

CAEN

BECAUSE OF THE JABOS AND THE ACTIVITIES OF THE RESISTANCE AGAINST THE RAILWAY LINES THEY ARE ARRIVING MUCH TOO LATE.

ARROMANCHES

BAYEUX

CAEN

THE 2ND SS PANZER LEFT TOULOUSE IN THE EVENING OF JUNE 6,... IT HASN'T ARRIVED IN NORMANDY YET!

I PITY THE BOYS! THEY MUST HAVE HAD ENOUGH OF IT!

AND WHAT ARE OUR SUBMARINES DOING?

IT SEEMS NONE HAS SUCCEEDED TO GET NEAR THE TRAFFIC AREA, HERR MARSHAL...

DONNERWETTER!

ON TUESDAY, JUNE 20, IN SOTTEVAST (BETWEEN CHERBOURG AND VALOGNES)...

WHAT'S THAT GIANT BUILDING SITE FOR?

TO LAUNCH A TERRIBLE WEAPON THE GERMANS SAID

51

V2- LAUNCHING BASE, SOTTEVAST (CHANNEL). PLAN OF THE SITE AS IT WOULD HAVE BEEN AT THE END OF THE CONSTRUCTION.

780 M.

51 M.

56 M.

N

PARTS CONSTRUCTED AT THE END OF JUNE 1944.

A SUPER FLYING BOMB?

THEY WERE TALKING ABOUT A GIANT TORPEDO!

WELL, IT WAS HIGH TIME WE ARRIVED!

WHAT DO WE SAY TO THE AMERICAN ULTIMATUM, HERR GENERAL?

NOTHING, FÖRSTER! WE'LL HOLD OUT AS LONG AS POSSIBLE ... TILL DEATH ...

THE GERMANS HAD TRANSFORMED CHERBOURG, ALREADY FORTIFIED IN THE 19th CENTURY, INTO A STRONGHOLD CROSSED WITH TUNNELS AND SUBTERRANEAN BATTERIES. SINCE JUNE 23, GENERAL COLLINS' TROOPS HAVE OCCUPIED THE HEIGHTS THAT DOMINATE THE CITY.

GENERAL KARL VON SCHLIEBEN CONDUCTS THE LAST COMBATS FROM HIS UNDERGROUND HQ IN VILLA MAURICE IN OCTEVILLE.

THE BASES ARE FALLING ONE BY ONE, HERR GENERAL ... THE SURVIVORS PILE UP HERE IN OUR SHELTER ...

AND THE ROULE FORTRESS?

STILL HOLDING OUT ... BUT FOR HOW LONG?

BAM!

I DON'T WANT TO DIE IN THIS HOLE, WILHEM!

CALM DOWN, OLD FELLOW!

54

MONDAY, JUNE 26...

THE ROULE FORTRESS HAS SURRENDERED TONIGHT, HERR GENERAL... THE FORT DES FLAMANDS IS ON FIRE AND THE FOURCHES BULWARK HAS FALLEN!

THE AMERICANS ARE THROWING GRENADES IN OUR AIR TUBES.... OUR SHELTER IS A HELL WITH UNBREATHABLE AIR...

MM...

LIEUTENANT OHMSEN HAS REQUESTED TO BE RECEIVED BY ADMIRAL HENNECKE...

I PROPOSE SHOOTING AT THE ENEMY ON THE HEIGHTS... I DID THAT IN MARCOUF!

BRILLIANT IDEA! LET'S CALL THE BATTERIES OF CAP DE LA HAGUE...

THE BATTERIES OF AUDERVILLE HAVE BEEN BOMBED SO MUCH THAT THEY WOULDN'T HAVE ANY PRECISION! YOUR PLAN WON'T WORK, LIEUTENANT! A PITY!

EARLY IN THE AFTERNOON...

VON SCHLIEBEN AND HENNECKE ARE SURRENDERING... WARN GENERAL EDDY AND "BLITZ JOE"[1]...

(1) GENERAL COLLINS' NICKNAME

THERE THEY ARE!

WHEREAS ON TUESDAY, JUNE 27, AT THE MARINE HQ, WEST OF PARIS...

WHAT? ONE OF OUR MARINE OFFICERS HAS THE KEY TO IGNITE ALL MINES ROUND CHERBOURG?

YES, ADMIRAL

HE'S BEEN ABLE TO GET BACK TO FORT WEST[2] WITH A SAILING SHIP AND TWO WHALE SLOOPS! THE AMERICANS MUST BE FURIOUS!

(2) AT THE EXIT OF THE PORT...

THE NEWS (LARGELY EXAGGERATED BY THE O.K.W.) DRIVES "BLITZ JOE" MAD...

BAF

BOMBED DURING THREE DAYS, THE BUNKER WITH THE FAMOUS KEY IS FINALLY SMASHED AND HENCE THE INSTALLATION THAT COULD HAVE BLOCKED THE PORT.

I WANT FORT WEST SMASHED WITH MORTAR-SHELLS! EXECUTE!

53

ON THURSDAY, JUNE 29, VON RUNDSTEDT AND ROMMEL, CALLED FOR BY ADOLF HITLER, DRIVE TO GERMANY.

POOR DOLLMANN[1]... THE FALL OF CHERBOURG HAS BEEN FATAL TO HIM... A HEART ATTACK STRUCK HIM DOWN LAST NIGHT...

A HEART ATTACK? I DIDN'T KNOW HE WAS ILL...

[1] CHIEF OF THE 7th GERMAN ARMY (THE ARMY OF NORMANDY).

HIS CHIEF OF STAFF PHONED ME THE NEWS THIS MORNING[2]...

[2] IN FACT, GENERAL DOLLMANN COMMITTED SUICIDE.

THE NEXT DAY IN CHERBOURG...

RADIO CHERBOURG... WE CAN REPORT THAT TODAY THE LAST GERMAN RESISTANCE POSTS HAVE BEEN DESTROYED...

... STILL, THE CITY LOOKS SAD IN SPITE OF THE VICTORY... INDEED, THE ENEMY HAS CAUSED ITS SYSTEMATIC DESTRUCTION...

ONCE ONE OF THE MOST MODERN PORTS IN THE WORLD, CHERBOURG IS NOW A DEVASTATED CITY! THAT WAS THE NEWS BY IMLAY WATTS...

SOMEWHERE ELSE IN THE CITY...

Arge PFALZ
LATSCHA
Z
MICHEELS COLLIGNON
RAEBEL-WERKE
Mia.
Arge PFALZ

HELLO... I'D LIKE TO SEE A MILITARY CHIEF... I'VE FOUND A PLATE ON A FRAGMENT OF A PLANE...

THE AIRCRAFT CRASHED NEAR OUR FARM ON APRIL 26... I'VE NOTED DOWN THE DATE!

VERY GOOD, BOY... IT'S THE ID PLATE OF AN ENGLISH PLANE...

...WE'LL SEND IT TO THE R.A.F.!

54

SATURDAY, JULY 1, IN LA ROCHE-GUYON...

WHAT'S HAPPENED WHILE I WAS WITH THE FÜHRER?

MONTGOMERY'S OFFENSIVE WAS HALTED AT THE ODON, BUT WE'LL NEVER BE ABLE TO GET TO THE SEA AGAIN, HERR MARSHAL ...

OUR LOSSES OF MEN AND MATERIAL ARE SO HIGH THAT THE UNIT CHIEFS ASK FOR THE WITHDRAWAL OF THE FRONT-LINE ...

SPEIDEL! I AGREE! INFORM VON RUNDSTEDT!

THE MARSHAL TOO ACCEPTS THAT PROPOSAL AND TRANSMITS IT TO THE O.K.W. ... SOMEWHAT LATER ...

SORRY, HERR FELD-MARSCHALL, THE FÜHRER TURNS DOWN YOUR REQUEST,... ANY WITHDRAWAL IS FORBIDDEN!

IN THAT CASE HE MAY RELIEVE ME OF MY DUTY AS COMMANDER!

THE NEXT DAY...

THEY FIRED HIM?

HE WAS STRICT BUT NOT BAD!

I COME TO TELL YOU THAT THE "BOSS" HAS BEEN DISMISSED...

... FOR "HEALTH REASONS"! IT MAKES ME SICK!

WHO'S REPLACING HIM?

VON KLUGE!... BUT... HUSH, WILL YOU?

MARSHAL VON KLUGE

AT THE SAME TIME, NEAR THE FRONT...

FEELS GOOD TO FLY!

DAN, THE "WING"(1) WANTS TO SEE YOU... HURRY!

(1) SQUADRON LEADER

THEY FOUND THE ID PLATE AND THE DEBRIS OF YOUR BROTHER'S "SPIT" NEAR CHERBOURG. FROM NOW ON HE'S OFFICIALLY DEAD, SERGEANT ...

NOW I'LL HAVE TO TAKE CARE OF MY PARENTS...

55

AFTER THE CAPTURE OF CHERBOURG, THE AMERICAN TROOPS RETURN SOUTH. BUT THE PROGRESS FROM CARENTAN ON IS DIFFICULT...

WHAT A PLACE! HEDGES, SMALL FIELDS, HILLOCKS EVERYWHERE...

HA! IT'S NOT TEXAS, CHARLIE...

IN ENGLAND, WHERE GENERAL PATTON IS GETTING READY TO EMBARK FOR NORMANDY WITH THE 3RD ARMY...

GENTLEMEN, AT LAST WE LEAVE FOR THE WAR! I FORETELL THAT YOUR NAMES WILL ENTER HISTORY OR ELSE THEY'LL BE FOUND ON THE LISTS OF THE DECEASED. THANK YOU!

NO KRAUTS ANYWHERE. WE WON'T STAY HERE FOR TEN YEARS!

PiuuuwW

PANG!

FROM TUESDAY, JULY 4, "THE BATTLE OF CAEN" STARTS. THE "REGINA" ATTACKS NORTHWEST OF THE CITY...

SUDDENLY...

CAREFUL! PANZERS!

I MUST GET ONE!

I'LL WAIT FOR IT TO PASS... IF ITS TANK IS NOT FULL, THE FUEL VAPOURS WILL IGNITE EASILY!

YEP!... BUT THERE'S ANOTHER TANK...

I'LL ZERO IN ON THAT ONE!

56

TEUFEL!

BOUM!

HIT!

BOF!

BEAUTIFUL SHOT, WILLIE!

BUT... IT'S THE SS WHO KILLS OUR PRISONERS! FORWARD!

IN THE SECOND GERMAN TANK...

THEY'RE CHASING AFTER THE USTUF! ABOUT-TURN! MOVE!

CANADIAN TANKS STRAIGHT AHEAD! BACK, HURRY!

MEANWHILE, WILLIE AND TERRANCE DON'T LET KERNER GO...

!!

CLAC!

WATCH OUT, WILLIE! HE'S GOING TO ... TAKE COVER!

WHAM!

LATER, IN BRIGADEFÜHRER KURT MEYER'S FORMER HQ...

THAT SS ESCAPED! HE'S LUCKY!

THE TIDE MAY TURN...

NEW BOMBINGS HAVE PAVED THE WAY FOR THE FINAL ATTACK ON CAEN...

AND, ON JULY 9...

OUR POSITIONS HAVE BEEN DESTROYED ONE BY ONE, HERR BRIGADEFÜHRER... WHAT ARE THE ORDERS?

WE RETREAT... I KNOW! THOSE ARE NOT THE ORDERS, BUT I SAY: RETREAT!

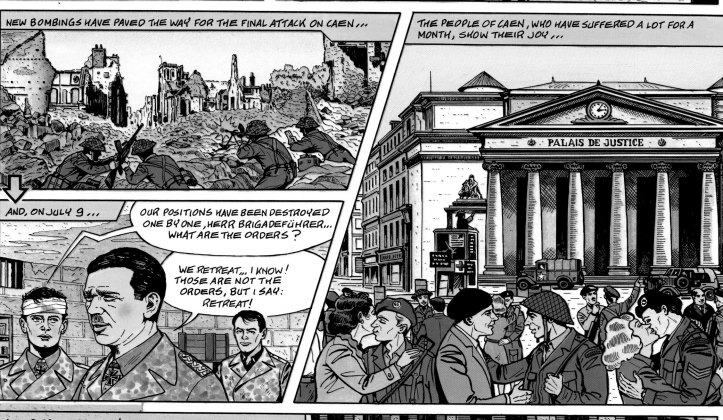

THE PEOPLE OF CAEN, WHO HAVE SUFFERED A LOT FOR A MONTH, SHOW THEIR JOY...

PALAIS DE JUSTICE

ALLIED SOLDIERS, V.A.D.'S AND MEMBERS OF FRED SCAMARONI'S RESISTANCE FRATERNIZE...

...ANYWAY, IN SPITE OF THE VICTORY THEY WOULD HAVE TO WAIT FOR JULY 18 BEFORE FIRING ON THE CITY AND THE THREATS OF GERMAN COUNTERATTACKS WOULD STOP.

LONG LIVE AMERICA!

LONG LIVE DE GAULLE!

THIS IS RADIO CHERBOURG... ON THIS FRIDAY, JULY 14, THE FRENCH NATIONAL HOLIDAY IS CELEBRATED WITH SPECIAL ENTHUSIASM IN THE LIBERATED CITIES...

IN CHERBOURG, WITH ALLIED FLAGS PUT OUT EVERYWHERE, AMERICAN TROOPS AND FRENCH MARINE FIREMEN ARE MARCHING SIDE BY SIDE...

INHABITANTS OF CHERBOURG PROUDLY SHOW THE CROSS OF LORRAINE, WHICH IS THE SHOULDER BADGE OF THE 79th AMERICAN DIVISION[1] THE ONE THAT HAS TAKEN THE ROULE FORTRESS!

(1) THIS DIVISION HAD FOUGHT IN LORRAINE DURING THE GREAT WAR.

AFTER THE "HEDGEROW WAR", THE AMERICANS FIGHT FIERCELY TO THE NORTH OF SAINT-LÔ.

TAC TAC TAC TAC TAC

GERMAN PARAS!

BUT A LITTLE FURTHER, BEHIND A SLOPE....

WOUFF

WHAM

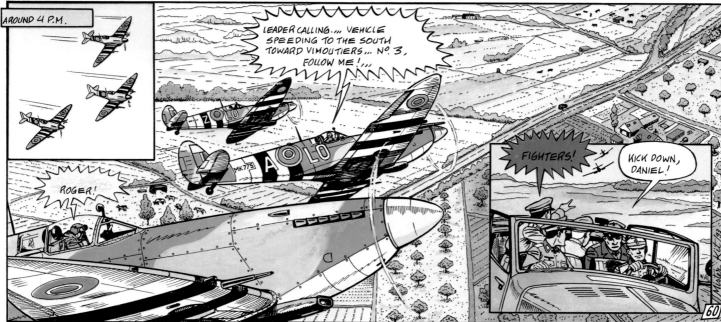

THE FIGHTERS BELONG TO THE 602nd R.A.F. SQUADRON. THEIR LEADER "CHRIS" LE ROUX LAUNCHES THE ATTACK...

FASTER, DANIEL! TRY TO REACH THE VILLAGE!

DIVE!

ACHTUNG! (1)

VRROOOAWW

(1) ATTENTION!

THE SPIT'S CANONS EACH FIRE 10 MORTARSHELLS PER SECOND...

BAM BAM BAM
BAM
BAM
BAM
BAM

ROMMEL AND HIS DRIVER ARE HIT...

piiiiww

piiiw

WELL DONE, CHRIS! YOU GOT THEM!

SQUADRON LEADER J.J. "CHRIS" LE ROUX (D.F.C. & 2 BARS), SOUTH AFRICAN PILOT, DISAPPEARED ON AUGUST 29, 1944.

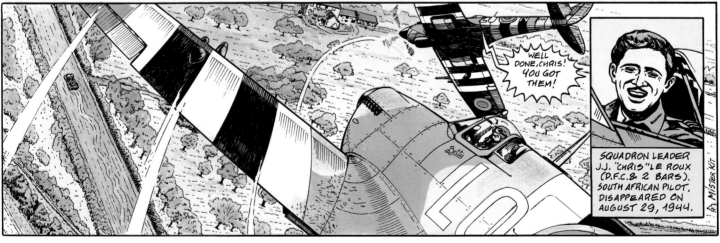

LATER, IN A HOUSE NEARBY...

WELL... BADLY BEATEN UP, YOUR MAN!

THERE'S A CAR COMING... STOP IT...

A MECHANIC OF THE GERMAN ARMY WHO HAPPENED TO COME BY TRANSPORTS THE INJURED TO LIVAROT...

Pharmacie

THE ONE YOU CALL FELDMARSCHALL WILL DIE IF HE'S NOT RUSHED TO HOSPITAL...

LET'S GO, THEN!

61

63

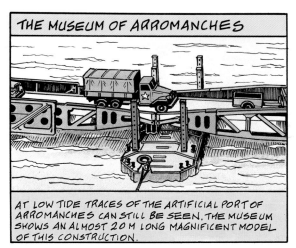

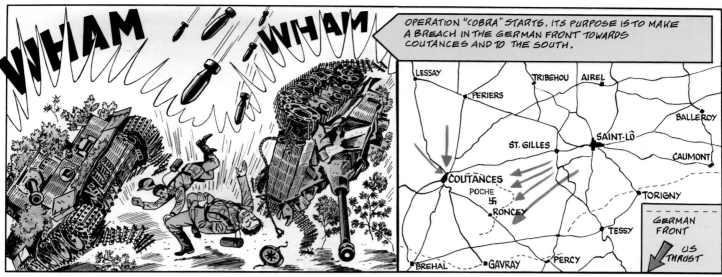

WHAM WHAM

OPERATION "COBRA" STARTS. ITS PURPOSE IS TO MAKE A BREACH IN THE GERMAN FRONT TOWARDS COUTANCES AND TO THE SOUTH.

THE BREAKTHROUGH SUCCEEDS AND ON JULY 28, THE US TANKS ARE AT THE GATES OF COUTANCES ...

DON'T CRY, ARLETTE! WE'VE LEFT THE COMBAT ZONE! FOR US THE WAR IS OVER!

AT THE HQ OF THE 11th CORPS OF GERMAN PARACHUTISTS, NEAR PERCY ...

WHAT ARE YOU DOING HERE?

I'M LT.-COLONEL VON KLUGE, THE FELDMARSCHALL'S SON, GENERAL.

MY FATHER ...ER... THE FELDMARSCHALL WANTS YOU TO HOLD OUT AND ASKS THAT THE TANKS ....

WHICH TANKS?

THE PANZER LEHR DOESN'T EXIST ANYMORE AND THE FIGHTERS WILL TRANSFORM THE REST OF THE OTHER UNITS INTO SMOKING WRECKS COLONEL!

ALL THESE ORDERS 'VE BEEN CONCEIVED BY PEOPLE WHO HAVEN'T THE FOGGIEST IDEA OF THE SITUATION!

MOREOVER, WE EXPECTED AN ATTACK TOWARD THE EAST AND THE SOUTH-EAST AND THAT DEVIL PATTON PUSHES TOWARD THE SOUTH-WEST, FROM THE OTHER SIDE

HE'LL BE IN AVRANCHES BY THE END OF THE MONTH!

INDEED, ON MONDAY, JULY 31, AVRANCHES IS TAKEN AND PASSED BY, PATTON IS RESTLESS ...

HAVE A BULLDOZER CLEAN THIS UP! NOTHING MUST DELAY OUR ADVANCE!

ON TUESDAY, AUGUST 1, IN THE UTAH AREA ...

TAKE A BREATHER, BOYS! WE'RE HOME! IN FRANCE!

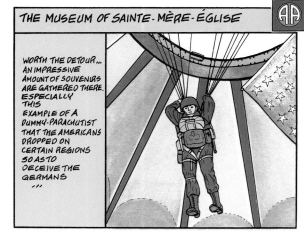

WORTH THE DETOUR ... AN IMPRESSIVE AMOUNT OF SOUVENIRS ARE GATHERED THERE. ESPECIALLY THIS EXAMPLE OF A DUMMY-PARACHUTIST THAT THE AMERICANS DROPPED ON CERTAIN REGIONS SO AS TO DECEIVE THE GERMANS ...

THE 2nd FRENCH TANK DIVISION (2ème D.B.) WILL FIGHT TOGETHER WITH PATTON'S 3rd ARMY ...

ACTION! THE PERSON WITH THE BERET IS GENERAL LECLERC ... THE OTHER ONE, WALKER.

UNDER THE COMMAND OF GENERAL LECLERC, THE 2ème D.B. GOES TO THE FRONT IMMEDIATELY. SOME DAYS LATER, THE BELGIAN BRIGADE LANDS IN ARROMANCHES ...

COLONEL PIRON.

UNDER THE ORDERS OF COLONEL PIRON THE BRIGADE WILL FIGHT UNDER THE COMMAND OF GENERAL GALE TO THE EAST OF THE ORNE ...

I PREFER HAVING ARRIVED BY BOAT TO THIS, REALLY!

YEP! IT MUST HAVE BEEN A SERIOUS CRASH!

ON SUNDAY, AUGUST 6, IN ST-GERMAIN-EN-LAYE ...

FELDMARSCHALL VON KLUGE CALLING ... GIVE ME THE FÜHRER ... OH, IT'S YOU, JODL ... ACCORDING TO THE O.K.W.'S ORDERS ...

... I'VE BEEN ABLE TO GATHER 400 TANKS AND 300 AIRPLANES. I WILL ATTACK TOMORROW!

NOT AT ALL, HERR MARSCHALL! YOU WILL ONLY TAKE THE COUNTER-OFFENSIVE ON AUGUST 8!

VILLEDIEU ST SEVER •CONDÉ
•BRÉCEY
•AVRANCHES •FLERS
MORTAIN•

•FOUGERES

IF I WAIT ONE MORE DAY, THE FIGHTERS WILL BECOME AWARE OF MY TANKS!

THESE ARE THE FÜHRER'S ORDERS!

THE O.K.W. WANTED TO SLOW DOWN THE GERMAN BREAKTHROUGH TO ENSNARE THE MAXIMUM NUMBER OF ENEMY TROOPS...

NEIN! I WILL ATTACK TOMORROW AFTER ALL!

AT THE SAME TIME, IN THE CITY...

THE GERMAN "GREY MICE" TAKE TO THEIR HEELS...GOOD SIGN!

YES, AND THE "FRITZ" (1) HAVE REQUISITIONED ALL THE BICYCLES!

(1) GERMANS

THE NEXT DAY, AT DAYBREAK...

I CAN'T SEE ANYTHING!

DON'T MOAN! THE FIGHTERS WILL LEAVE US IN PEACE!

OUR AIRPLANES WILL TAKE CARE OF THEIR FIGHTERS!

THE OFFENSIVE TOWARDS THE WEST (MORTAIN, AVRANCHES AND THE SEA) IS INTENDED TO CUT OFF AMERICAN SUPPLIES. BUT BY NOON...

THE GERMAN AIRPLANES HAD ALL BEEN PINNED TO THE GROUND OR DESTROYED AT TAKE-OFF...

WHAM

THE GERMAN COUNTER-ATTACK FAILS AND THE FÜHRER DOES NOT HIDE HIS RAGE...

VON KLUGE HAS DELIBERATELY MADE THE OPERATION A FAILURE! MY ORDERS WERE CLEAR ENOUGH, THOUGH!

66

IN ST. GERMAIN-EN-LAYE...

IT'S A BAD DAY, MEN!

YOU BET! THE AMERICAN AIRPLANES ARE MACHINE-GUNNING ALL OUR TRAINS...

THEY SAY THAT PATTON'S TANKS ARE PUSHING INTO BRITTANY. THAT DOESN'T HELP EITHER!

EVEN IF PATTON'S ADVANCE IS DEVASTATING, THE GERMAN FRONT CAN RESIST WELL TO THE SOUTH OF CAUMONT AND VILLERS-BOCAGE. MEANWHILE SGT. RILEY IN HIS TANK...

IT'S TOO CALM... I DON'T LIKE IT!

ACHTUNG! A SHERMAN!

WOUFF

BAM

FEUER!

HURRY UP! EVERYTHING'S GOING TO EXPLODE! QUICK!

THE REST OF MY CREW IS TRAPPED IN THE TANK!

IN THE HOUSE OPPOSITE, FROM THE OTHER SIDE OF THE STREET...

DOES HE MEAN THAT THE KRAUTS ARE UPSTAIRS?

THROW A GRENADE... I'LL GO UPSTAIRS...

67

Since August 7 the Canadians have attacked at the south of Caen, terrifying bombings demoralize the Germans ... and "Panzer" Meyer ...

SOMEWHAT LATER...

IT IS REALLY WHAT I HAD FORESEEN: THE GUNS OF THE AMERICAN FLEET HAVE FLATTENED CINTHEAUX (*)...

(*) VILLAGE ON THE CAEN-FALAISE ROAD...

WE'RE GOING TO SETTLE THERE... WITTMANN'S "TIGERS" WILL COVER OUR FLANKS... GO AND WARN HIM, KERNER!

VROOO

THE 28TH CANADIAN REGIMENT'S ATTACKS COME UP AGAINST THE DEFENSIVE LINE INSTALLED BY "PANZER-MEYER"...

BAM
TAC TAC TAC

MICHAËL WITTMANN WANTS SOME MORE TANKS AS HUNTING TROPHIES...

THAT'S FOR ME!

FORWARD!

BUT THERE ARE FIVE OF THEM!

SURPRISE IS OUR ADVANTAGE! FULL THROTTLE!

WITTMANN MEETS HIS DEATH ON AUGUST 8, 1944, AT THE END OF THE DAY, DURING THIS ENCOUNTER...

HIS MORTAL REMAINS WERE NOT RECOVERED UNTIL MAY 1983.

IN CREULLY CASTLE (NOT FAR FROM MONTGOMERY'S HQ)...

THIS IS THE BBC, CHESTER WILMOT ON THE MICROPHONE. TODAY, AUGUST 15, AFTER AERIAL AND NAVAL BOMBARDMENT, THE FRANCO-AMERICAN FORCES HAVE LANDED IN THE SOUTH OF FRANCE, IN PROVENCE...

WHEREAS IN THE CASTLE AT LA ROCHE-GUYON...

WHAT'S HAPPENING?

WHERE ARE YOU GOING WITH THAT?

HIDE THESE OBJECTS. YOU NEVER KNOW WITH THE LATEST EVENTS...

IN ST.-GERMAIN-EN-LAYE...

YOU MUST GO TO BEAUVAIS "ALL BY YOURSELVES"? IS THAT A JOKE?

NO, BUT THE IDEA OF A LONG MARCH. REST ASSURED...

...I'VE STOLEN THE AIDE-DE-CAMP'S BIKE... THAT'S FOR THE THOUSANDS OF TIMES HE HAS SHOUTED ME DOWN!

THE NEWS OF THE LANDING IN PROVENCE, ALONG WITH THE PREDICTABLE COLLAPSE OF THE FRONT IN NORMANDY, UNLEASHES A MURDEROUS MADNESS IN SOME GERMAN UNITS.

SUMMARY EXECUTIONS OF RESISTANCE FIGHTERS, HOSTAGES AND SUSPECTS MULTIPLY...

THESE OUTRAGES PROVOKE BLIND RETALIATION...

A FRITZ!

SOLDIER DOLF SCHÖRNER LEAVES ST.-GERMAIN-EN-LAYE...

AFTER THE WAR, I'LL COME BACK HERE... AS A TOURIST...

71

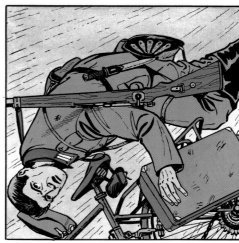

ON AUGUST 16, COMMANDO 4 IS ORDERED TO ATTACK...

IT SEEMS WE'RE PREPARING A HUGE OFFENSIVE TO CRUSH THE KRAUTS...

THEY'VE TOLD US SO EVER SINCE D-DAY!

LE SAULT IS HURT...

AAAH!

FLUSH OUT THAT SNIPER!

ICH ERGEBE MICH [1]

BASTARD!

(1) I SURRENDER

I DON'T SURRENDER TO FRENCHMEN!

YOU DON'T EH!

BOF

LEAVE HIM ALONE! HE'LL PULL THROUGH! EVACUATE HIM!

MEANWHILE, IN GERMANY ...

YES, IT'S ME, MANFRED ROMMEL, COLONEL!

YOUR FATHER HAS LEFT THE FRENCH HOSPITAL ... HE HAS RETURNED ... YOU HAVE A LEAVE PASS.

LATER IN THE FELDMARSCHALL'S HOUSE ...

SINCE THE FAILED ATTEMPT ON THE FÜHRER[1] THEY'VE WANTED TO ELIMINATE ME ...

BUT ...

NO QUESTIONS, MANFRED! KEEP THIS WITH YOU AND TAKE CARE OF YOUR MOTHER!

AT HITLER'S ORDERS, THE GESTAPO WILL FORCE ROMMEL TO COMMIT SUICIDE IN OCTOBER 1944.

[1] ON JULY 20, 1944.

ON FRIDAY, AUGUST 18, IN LA ROCHE-GUYON, JUST BEFORE DAYBREAK ...

AT THE MOMENT WHEN LA ROCHE-GUYON IS ALREADY UNDER AMERICAN GUNFIRE, I BID YOU FAREWELL ... AS YOU KNOW, THE FÜHRER DEPRIVED ME OF MY COMMAND YESTERDAY ...

I HAVE UNDERTAKEN TO DIRECT THE 7TH ARMY'S WITHDRAWAL BEHIND THE RIVER SEINE BUT I'M AFRAID IT'S ALREADY TOO LATE! GOOD LUCK, GENTLEMEN!

MARSHAL VON KLUGE WILL POISON HIMSELF THE SAME DAY.

BETWEEN AUGUST 18 AND 20, THE "FALAISE POCKET" CLOSES AGAIN ... THE 120,000 MEN WHO RUN FROM THE ENCIRCLEMENT, FIRST WITHDRAW IN GOOD ORDER, THEN IN EXTREME CONFUSION BECAUSE OF THE BOMBINGS ...

IF YOU GET OUT, WRITE TO MY HOME!

OK! YOU KNOW WE'VE ONLY GOT A CORRIDOR 8 KM WIDE TO ESCAPE FROM THE CARNAGE?

YES, I DO!

73

ON SUNDAY, AUGUST 20, WITH THE REMAINS OF THE 12TH PANZER SS, NORTHEAST OF FALAISE, "PANZER" MEYER...

GENTLEMEN! I HAVE THE ORDER TO WITHDRAW OUR DIVISION TO THE REAR LINE OF THE FRONT... WE'LL TRY TO CROSS THE RIVER DIVES IN SAINT-LAMBERT, AT NOON SHARP!

YOUR "DIVISION"... YOU MEAN YOUR BRATS TRANSFORMED INTO KILLING MACHINES! IT'S RIDICULOUS!

IT'S US WHO ARE LAUGHING! YOU LOOK LIKE A CLOWN WITH YOUR GIRL'S BIKE!

CLOWN? YOU'LL SEE...

HERE OUR TANKS ARE RUNNING OVER CORPSES TO ESCAPE FROM THIS HELL... YOU WILL NOT EVEN BE A DEAD BUT A MISSING PERSON!

THAT'LL DO, KERNER!... AND YOU, TAKE YOURSELF OFF!... GET READY, GENTLEMEN!

IN SAINT-LAMBERT, WHERE THE BRIDGES OVER THE DIVES ARE HELD BY THE CANADIANS...

BUT...

GIVE A SIGNAL TO "PANZER" MEYER!

TAC TAC TAC TAC

BAM

TAC TAC TAC TAC

74

THE 2ⁿᵈ PANZER, THE 10ᵗʰ PANZER SS, THE 116ᵗʰ PANZER AND OTHER UNITS RUSH TOWARD THE BRIDGE OVER THE DIVES, TO CLEAR THE WAY. VEHICLES, HORSES AND INJURED ARE DUMPED INTO THE RAVINE ...

ON AUGUST 20, THE "POCKET" IS CLOSED, THE ARTILLERY AND THE AIR FORCE BLUDGEON THE ENSNARED TROOPS ...

LOOK AT THAT, DAN ... KILOMETRES OF CORPSES AND BURNING WRECKS!

M. Kit.

I HOPE THE WORLD WILL NEVER SEE SUCH A HORROR AGAIN!

VROAWWW

FILL UP THE MOTORCYCLE!

THERE'S NO MORE FUEL, HERR USTUF ...

FIND SOME!

WHERE ARE YOU GOING, KERNER?

I'M LEAVING YOU, HERR BRIGADEFÜHRER! WE'VE LOST THE WAR!

YOU'RE CRAZY!

NO, HERR BRIGADEFÜHRER ... DEAD, INJURED AND PRISONERS IN ALL WE'VE LOST HALF A MILLION MEN ... WE WON'T RECOVER FROM THAT!

VROM VROM

75

77

THE WAR WILL SOON END AND I CAN'T DO ANYTHING, WHAT WILL BECOME OF ME?

...SO I'LL GET BACK TO DO THE ONLY THING I'VE LEARNED... FAREWELL, BRIGADEFÜHRER!

KERNER!

VROOP

VRAOWW

FURTHER, NEAR THE POSITIONS HELD BY THE CANADIANS, NORTHEAST OF SAINT-LAMBERT...

!!

VROOOAW

IT'S HIM!

IT'S THAT SS!

HE'S RIDING STRAIGHT INTO THE ZONE THE ARTILLERY IS WIPING OUT!

VROAAAW

WOUFF

76

THE "BATTLE OF FALAISE" ENDS ON TUESDAY MORNING, AUGUST 22, AND THE SAME DAY...

TO ALL UNITS... FINALLY WE HAVE THE ORDERS TO GET GOING TO PARIS...

THE 2ème D.B. AVANCES ON RAMBOUILLET...

SEND A MESSAGE TO THE PARISIANS WHO HAVE TAKEN UP ARMS AGAINST THE ENEMY: WE ARE COMING! DON'T GIVE UP!

FOR THEIR PART THE BELGIAN BRIGADE HAS LIBERATED CABOURG, DEAUVILLE, HONFLEUR,... AND GETS READY TO ATTACK LE HAVRE...

COMMANDO 4 TAKES PONT-L'ÉVÊQUE WHICH THE GERMANS HAVE SET ON FIRE...

THERE ARE ENGLISH PRISONERS IN THE BURNING FELDKOMMAN-DATUR! IT'S NEARBY!

YOU'RE ARRIVING JUST IN TIME, BOYS!

KOMMANDATUR

WHERE ARE YOU FROM?

FROM OUISTREHAM! IT'S BEEN TEN WEEKS NOW THAT WE'VE BEEN FIGHTING CEASELESSLY AND WITH ALMOST NO SLEEP...

WE WERE ONLY 177 FRENCHMEN TO LAND „ BUT WE DESERVED OUR PLACES!

79

MEANWHILE, ON THE BANKS OF THE SEINE, SOUTH OF ROUEN...

YOUR NAME?... MEN AND VEHICLES?...

BRIGADEFÜHRER KURTMEYER, 12th PANZER SS,... 280 MEN SAVED AND 18 VEHICLES OF WHICH 10 TANKS...

THANKS TO FLOATING BRIDGES (DISASSEMBLED AND HIDDEN DURING THE DAY) THE TROOPS THAT ESCAPED FROM THE FALAISE POCKET CONTINUE THEIR WITHDRAWAL...

IS THAT ALL?

SADLY!

THEN YOU CAN LEAVE, HERR BRIGADEFÜHRER... GOOD LUCK!

GOOD LUCK, TO YOU TOO!

THE NEXT DAY AT BASE B7

WHERE'S YOUR CHIEF? I WANT TO HAVE A WORD WITH HIM. I'M FED UP WITH YOUR STUNTS...

...THEY FRIGHTEN MY COWS AND IT AIN'T GOOD FOR THE MILK!

VRROOOO

...BUT GIVE THIS BOTTLE TO YOUR MEN... WITH ALL MY PRAISE, BECAUSE I'VE HAD ENOUGH OF YOUR WAR ...

OF "OUR" WAR?

THE MUSEUM OF THE RANGERS

ATTACK ON LA POINTE DU HOC

LT.-COLONEL J.E. RUDDER

LOCATED IN GRANDCAMP-MAISY, THE SOUVENIRS OF THE FAMOUS EPIC OF THE RANGERS ARE WAITING FOR YOU.

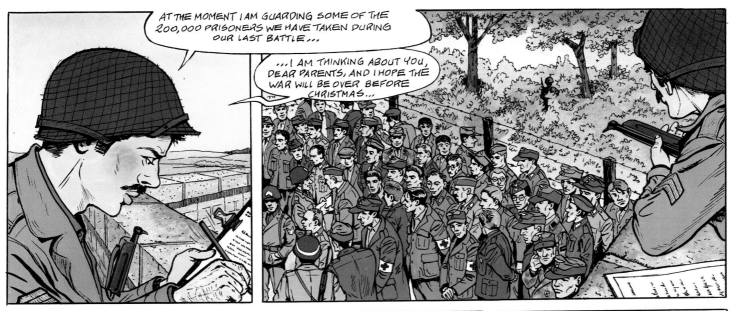

AT THE MOMENT I AM GUARDING SOME OF THE 200,000 PRISONERS WE HAVE TAKEN DURING OUR LAST BATTLE...

...I AM THINKING ABOUT YOU, DEAR PARENTS, AND I HOPE THE WAR WILL BE OVER BEFORE CHRISTMAS...

IN FORMIGNY...

HOW ARE YOU, ADRIEN?

PHEW... THE TANKS HAVE DESTROYED MY CORN, MY ANIMALS ARE ILL AND I CAN'T FIND ANYTHING TO REPAIR MY FARM!

AFTER THE WAR WE'LL BECOME RICH, ADRIEN!

OH YES?

WE'LL EXPORT CAMEMBERT TO THE USA AND WE'LL IMPORT COLA-COLA!

JOINT BATTLES OF THE RESISTANCE AND THE 2ème D.B. ENABLE THE LIBERATION OF THE FRENCH CAPITAL ON AUGUST 25...

THE END OF THE "BATTLE OF NORMANDY" AND THE LIBERATION OF PARIS DO NOT MARK THE CONCLUSION OF THE BATTLES IN FRANCE. THE GERMAN ARMY HAS FORMED A COHERENT FRONT NORTH OF THE SEINE. THE WAR IS NOT OVER!

79

MUCH LATER, WHEN THE "BATTLE OF NORMANDY" ALREADY SEEMS TO BE REMOTE...

OUR COMMAND HASN'T WORKED TO PERFECTION... IF WE HAD ACCELERATED THE CLOSING OF THE FALAISE POCKET ...

... WE WOULD HAVE ELIMINATED FOR GOOD THE GERMAN ELITE TROOPS THAT WE FOUND AGAIN LATER!

IT'S TRUE, MONTY [1]... WE HAVEN'T SUCCEEDED IN PREVENTING THOSE UNITS FROM CROSSING THE SEINE EITHER...

[1] FRIENDLY NICKNAME OF MONTGOMERY.

BUT THOSE DIVISIONS HAVE LOST ALMOST ALL THEIR EQUIPMENT AND MORE PARTICULARLY THEY'VE LOST THEIR BEST SOLDIERS!

WE KNOW... THAT IS UNDENIABLE ... ER... DO YOU REMEMBER, MONTY, THAT RAIN-BEATEN NIGHT IN JUNE WHEN WE SAID ...

..."TUESDAY, JUNE 6 WILL BE D-DAY". WHO AMONG US DIDN'T FEAR DEFEAT?

THE END

SCRIPT: SERGE SAINT-MICHEL • DRAWINGS: MISTER KIT • COLOURS: MARTINE BOUTIN

AFTER THE BATTLE OF NORMANDY

1944

SEPTEMBER - liberation of Belgium ; the Americans enter on German territory near Aachen ; fierce battles in Alsace and Lorraine.

OCTOBER - Soviet offensive : the eastern border of Germany is reached ; liberation of Greece ; the Americans recover the Philippine Islands from the Japanese.

NOVEMBER - in France, liberation of Metz, Mulhouse and Strasbourg.

DECEMBER - failure of an impressive German counter-offensive in the Ardennes.

1945

JANUARY - irrepressible advance of the Soviet armies in central Europe and in eastern Germany.

FEBRUARY - in France, liberation of Colmar.

MARCH - collapse of the last German defensive lines east of the Rhine, in Bavaria and by the Oder ; American success in Iwo-Jima (Pacific) against the Japanese.

APRIL - in France, liberation of Royan ; the allies conquer northern Italy ; Americans and Russians join near Berlin.

8th MAY - German capitulation.

JUNE - the island of Okinawa is recovered from the Japanese.

JULY - American landing in Indonesia.

AUGUST - American atomic bombs on Hiroshima and Nagasaki.

1st SEPTEMBER - capitulation of Japan ; end of World War II.

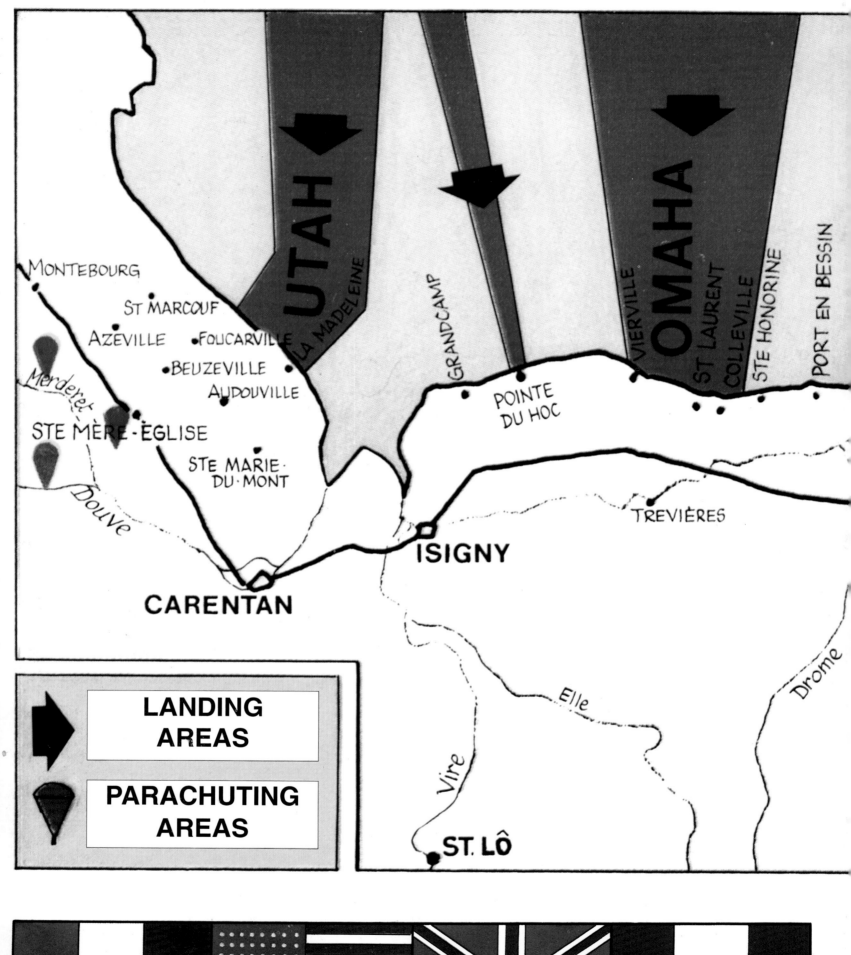

MONTEBOURG

ST MARCOUF

AZEVILLE · FOUCARVILLE

Merderet

·BEUZEVILLE ·

AUDOUVILLE

STE MÈRE-ÉGLISE

UTAH

LA MADELEINE

GRANDCAMP

VIERVILLE

OMAHA

ST LAURENT
COLLEVILLE
STE HONORINE
PORT EN BESSIN

Douve

STE MARIE·
DU·MONT

POINTE
DU HOC

CARENTAN

ISIGNY

TREVIÈRES

Elle

Drome

Vire

ST. LÔ

LANDING AREAS

PARACHUTING AREAS